# Painted out of

## THE STORY of
## ELLEN *and* ROLINDA SHARPLES

*for Malie Gethin
with love*

*Hazel*

x x

# HAZEL GOWER

*redcliffe*

First published in 2021 by Redcliffe Press Ltd
81g Pembroke Road, Bristol BS8 3EA

e: info@redcliffepress.co.uk
www.redcliffepress.co.uk
Follow us on Twitter @RedcliffePress

ISBN 978-1-911408-81-9

*British Library Cataloguing-in-Publication Data*
A catalogue record for this book is available from the British Library.

*Design and typesetting by Design Deluxe, Bath*
*Printed and bound by Hobbs the Printers Ltd, Totton*

Redcliffe Press Ltd is committed to being an environmentally friendly publisher.
This book is made from Forest Stewardship Council® certified paper.

*Front cover:* Rolinda Sharples, *The Artist and Her Mother,* 1816 Bristol Museums
Courtesy Bristol Culture

*Watercolours, Sharples family's residences:* All artworks by Hazel Gower,
photographs by Jon Rowley, https://jonrowleyphotography.com

*Newspaper excerpts:*
Courtesy of Bath Record Office, Archives and Local Studies
*Bristol Mercury* newspaper, 1845, © The British Library Board. All rights reserved.
With thanks to the British Newspaper Archive (www.britishnewspaperarchive.co.uk)

Photographs of Ellen's handwritten notes on paint preparation and colour-mixing are taken
from her recipes and notes book. RWA Library item 37, photographs by Tristan Pollard

# Contents

# Foreword

ELLEN SHARPLES WAS a truly remarkable woman. Born the same year as Napoleon Bonaparte; at the dawn of the age of steam, and six years before the American War of Independence, she witnessed a world changing at dizzying pace. By the time of her death in 1849, France had become an established Republic; industrialisation had transformed lives and landscapes across Britain and beyond, and Ellen herself had produced portraits of all five of the first Presidents of a country that was not only independent, but rapidly moving towards becoming a superpower.

Despite humble beginnings and all the disadvantages then laid on her gender, Ellen managed to combine raising a family (including her equally extraordinary daughter Rolinda) with being a highly successful professional artist – difficult enough even today. Through Ellen's support, Rolinda made the most of her talents, carving out a career that defied the conventions of her gender, painting not children and kittens, but sharply observed social documentaries of some of the key events of the time.

Bristol is fortunate that Ellen Sharples chose it as her final home city. Thanks to her, the city not only boasts one of the most beautiful art galleries in the country, its founding organisation led the way in providing parallel opportunities for artists, regardless of gender.

In 1844, having lost her beloved daughter and son James a few years earlier, Ellen was persuaded to donate £2000 – the equivalent of over £250,000 today – to the foundation of 'the Bristol Academy for the Promotion of Fine Arts', what is now the Royal West of England Academy (known as RWA). From the outset, there was an insistence on gender equality, leading to Bristol perhaps being the first city in the world to host life drawing classes that admitted women as well as men.

Founded initially as a peripatetic institution, the Academy needed a permanent home, and Ellen was part of the driving force that made it happen. Writing to one potential benefactor, she proclaimed:

> *If the Bristolians are only now liberal all preceding neglect of Art will be forgotten: an elegant edifice will arise – an ornament & honour to the city which in its walls will contain a succession of the various beauties of Art.*

Sadly, Ellen did not live to enjoy the elegant edifice for herself; however, it was her bequest of a further £4000, together with her family's collection of artworks, that finally saw Bristol gain its own Art Gallery and Art School, which opened to the public in 1858.

The institution Ellen brought into life has changed considerably over the years, and never more so than the year in which this book has been published, when – thanks to support from the National Lottery and many other sources – it will be made more accessible than at any time in its history. We are immensely proud that a core of equality runs through us from our earliest days, and that is thanks to our formidable founder.

We, the RWA, are hugely grateful to Hazel Gower for bringing Ellen's story into the spotlight, and for the many years of assiduous research that have underpinned her writing. We also thank the publishers, Redcliffe Press, who have celebrated and preserved Bristol's history for 45 years, from the founding vision of John Sansom to the brilliant current Director, Clara Hudson.

Ellen has been a hero and role model to me for many years. I hope this book will make her yours, too.

ALISON BEVAN
*Director, RWA (Royal West of England Academy)*

# Introduction

ELLEN AND ROLINDA SHARPLES are unique in the history of art: two generations of artists whose extraordinary lives tell a story quite outside the experience of most women of their time.

Ellen Sharples was a 17-year-old blacksmith's daughter from Lancashire when she married a little-known painter and inventor over twice her age. By the time her husband died in 1811 she was one of very few female professional artists on both sides of the Atlantic, and had painted the first five presidents of the United States. She trained her daughter, Rolinda, to become one of the first female narrative painters, and founded an Academy of Art where women could study on equal terms with men.

Such is the significance of the Sharples family in America that there are 45 of their portraits on permanent exhibition at the Independence National Historical Park in Philadelphia,[1] and many more of their works are in public and private collections throughout the US and UK. Some of their paintings may be viewed on the online collections website of Bristol Museums[2] and on the websites of the other galleries mentioned in this book.

Ellen gazes at us so demurely from beneath her bonnet in the few portraits of her that exist, but she possessed rare determination and resourcefulness. Her life as an artist and an entrepreneur broke with the conventions of her time and fortunately she kept a journal – it was often compiled after the event but allows fascinating access to her world – into which her artist daughter Rolinda's own diary notes were also copied. All the quotations in this book are taken from either this journal or Sharples family letters and papers, unless otherwise specified.

Her early work was as a skilled copyist of her husband James's work, but she made many of her own original portraits, which include the first portrait of Charles Darwin and one of the earliest paintings of a Native American in European art. As James pursued his passion for inventions, at home in Bath and throughout their travels Ellen worked ceaselessly to ensure her family's financial stability, at the same time educating her daughter and passing on her advanced ideas about female independence:

*I had frequently thought that every well educated female … should at least have the power … by the cultivation of some available talent … of obtaining the conveniences and some of the elegances of life.*

Ellen's daughter Rolinda, born only 18 years after Jane Austen, lived at a time when all female activities were extremely constrained, but she was fortunate in having an exceptional mother. Ellen's account of the home schooling of her daughter provides an intriguing insight into the world of a young girl growing up in a most unusual family during the Georgian era.

Trained in pastel portraiture, Rolinda became an innovator – it was virtually unheard of at that time for a female artist to have the ambition to tackle the subject matter she addressed. She documented contemporary events in large oil paintings featuring numerous figures, as well as making genre paintings of smaller groups and sustaining a remunerative portrait practice. Despite being isolated by her peers because of her gender, Rolinda lived as a professional artist in a provincial town, exhibiting widely and gaining national recognition by the end of her relatively short life.

Plate 1.1

**JAMES SHARPLES**

*Portrait of the Artist's Wife (Ellen Sharples)*

c.1786 | Pastel on paper | 24 x 18.5 cm, oval

Ashmolean Museum Oxford

CHAPTER ONE

# Beginnings, Marriage and Artistic Adventures in America, 1780s–1801

I T WAS THE YEAR 1786 that changed everything for 17-year-old Ellen Wallas. Her father – the blacksmith Rowland Wallas, a respected citizen and freeman of the City of Lancaster – died in the summer of 1786, buried on 16 June.[1] Ellen was left with her mother Margaret (née France) and her older brother Thomas. Within a few months she had met the man with whom she would share her future; on 6 January 1787 she married him, to be transported from provincial Lancashire into the precarious world of an aspiring portrait painter.

It has been suggested that Ellen came from a Quaker family,[2] but there is no evidence of this. In the first portrait we have of her (Plate 1.1), Ellen's dress does not reflect that of an eighteenth-century Quaker, and she married a Catholic in an Anglican church. She was born in Lancaster on 4 March 1769, her brother Thomas the year before; her parents had married on 8 November 1767. In the eighteenth century a blacksmith was a central figure in the local community and often something of a businessman, so Ellen may have inherited this quality from her father. Margaret and Rowland clearly had ambitions for their only daughter and somehow gave her that rare thing for a girl from her background – an education. Ellen mentions in her journal having attended an unnamed Manchester boarding school.

## EDUCATION AND MARRIAGE

Few girls from a working-class family could read or write at that time, and anyone with a little education could open a school. The writer Hannah More and her sisters taught at a school for young ladies at 60 Park Street in Bristol – a city that would play a large role in Ellen and Rolinda's lives – and a few ladies' boarding schools existed in Manchester in the 1770s and '80s, where a small number of pupils were presided over by a widow or an unmarried woman.

The emphasis in such places was on the cultivation of genteel social accomplishments, designed to prepare young women for marriage. Morals and manners were the order of the day, sometimes including instruction in washing fine linen and clear starching, with lessons from an itinerant dancing master in the minuet, 'Louvre', allemande and reels. Fees charged for a year's board averaged around 13 guineas, with washing included. In 1771 a Miss Creswell advertised the curriculum of a school such as the one Ellen attended in the *Manchester Mercury*:

> *She proposes Boarding and Teaching Young Ladies English Grammar and various Kinds of Needlework, at fifteen Guineas a Year.*
>
> *No more than eighteen Ladies will be agreed for, as Miss Creswell will have the care of her pupils herself, except when they are with their Music, French, Dancing or Writing Masters.*
>
> *The Ladies are to spend their Time in this Manner: Rise at seven o'Clock; and after the Duty of Prayer and Breakfast, make ready their English Tasks: from nine 'till ten, Lessons on the Harpsichord; from ten 'till twelve, work and repeat their English Tasks; from twelve 'till one divert themselves; from half past one 'till half past two attend their French Master; from half past two 'till five work and read the following Authors, History of England, the Spectators, Adventurers, Lord Orrery's Letters, Mrs Pennington's Advice to her Daughters, Doddridges' Dialogues, Gays, Drapers, Croxall's and Dodsleys' Fables; from five 'till six Write and Accompt; six 'till eight divert themselves; sup at eight, and after evening Prayers retire to Bed, which will never be later than Nine o'Clock.*
>
> *It is hoped that a Life of Innocence and Instruction will form and unite the delightful Character of a pious Christian and an Accomplished Woman.*
>
> *N.B. Each pupil is desired to bring one Pair of Sheets and four Napkins.*
>
> *A servant is Wanted who understands Cooking.*

Ellen's school certainly gave her an enduring love of reading and learning, preparing her to become an exceptionally gifted teacher of her own daughter.

The location of the art class where Ellen first encountered her fascinating drawing master and future husband is uncertain; it may have been in Bath,[3] something of a marriage market at the time. The speed with which Margaret married off her daughter suggests some sense of urgency, although James Sharples may not have seemed an obvious choice: at 38 he was over twice Ellen's age, his second wife having just died in childbirth, leaving him with a baby son. But to the widow of a blacksmith he must have represented a significant step up the social ladder. James was from an old Lancashire Catholic family, his father a fellow of Brasenose College, Oxford and described as a gentleman.

From Ellen's expression in the above-mentioned portrait of her by James dated *c.*1786 (Plate 1.1), it seems to have been a love match: her gaze towards the artist is a tender one. On the back of the original frame was a small card inscribed:

> *Ellen Wallace [Wallas] of Lancaster, painted during the hours that he wooed the fair Ellen by that eminent artist in crayons Mr James Sharples, her happy husband. He wooed and won her for his bride.*[4]

Ellen is wearing a black ribbon on her bonnet in mourning for her father.

The marriage took place at the ancient parish church of the City of Lancaster, St Mary, on 6 January 1787. Ellen was described as a minor and was given away by her brother Thomas, who sadly died later that year, the witness one Sally Chorley.

## WHO WAS ELLEN'S HUSBAND?

James Sharples came from Woodplumpton, Lancashire, where a few old families had retained their Catholic faith after the Reformation. A later portrait from *c.*1802 shows what James might have looked like around the time he married Ellen (Plate 1.2). (Painted by his son, James Jnr, when was he just 13 or 14 and his father was in his mid-fifties, the picture seems to represent James Snr as a younger man, with only a hint of thinning hair and no lines or wrinkles.) Archives record his birthdate as 27 May 1748, although on his death certificate in 1811 he is described as being in his fifty-ninth year.

It has been suggested that he was sent to France in his youth to train as a priest but abandoned this to become an artist.[5] His son George from his first marriage was born in 1775; his second son Felix, born in 1786, was just a baby when he and Ellen met. Little is known of his first two wives. The second may have been an artist: an embroidery entitled *A Fruit Piece*, by a Mrs Sharpless (as James's surname was sometimes spelled), described as Embroideress to Her Majesty, was exhibited at the Royal Academy in 1783. George also became an artist and appears briefly at the end of Chapter 3.

James had plied his trade in several cities, living in Cambridge, London, Bath and Bristol. He first exhibited his work in 1774, in Liverpool, and first showed at London's Royal Academy in 1779 – in the latter showing four pictures including one drawing in 'crayon' (which we would now term pastel, see below). On 28 July 1781 *Felix Farley's Bristol Journal* announced:

*Mr Sharples, from Bath, portrait painter in oils and crayons, begs leave to inform the nobility and gentry of Bristol that he has removed from the Hartwells [Hotwells] to Mrs Jeffery's, Milliner, 28 Clare Street, where upwards of one hundred specimens of known characters may be seen.*

In 1783 he exhibited for a second time at the Royal Academy, from 45 Gerrard Street, Soho, and once more in 1785, giving his address as Grosvenor Place, Lock Hospital. Since this was a hospital for venereal disease he may have been under-taking a commission; it seems unlikely that he would disclose being a patient. Two oval pastel portraits date from this time: *Miss Davis* and *Miss Donaldson in a Black Hat*, with the latter inscribed on the back 'Sharples, Chapel Street, Grosvenor Place, London'.[6]

James considered himself to be as much an inventor as a portrait painter, and there are records of his ideas for 'steam carriages' and various proposals for mechanical devices.[7] He also sought out scientists for his portrait subjects. Ellen wrote ruefully of his preoccupation: 'Mr S. had greater talents for inventing than bringing his inventions into use – always more disposed to something new. A considerable sum had been spent in experiments …'

After their marriage Ellen and James lived on Everton Hill in Liverpool, where James's brother Henry was a timber merchant. The first home of their married life was

*situated on the summit of a hill commanding an extensive, varied and delightful prospect. On the left the town of Liverpool with its numerous spires, beyond which was a luxurious country terminated by the Welsh mountains. On the right from the main ocean, which was visible, the river Mersey flowed through a pleasing country to the town. On it were innumerable vessels, which with the windmills everywhere in action, gave life to the landscape.*

Later they rented Rainhill House, a few miles outside Liverpool, from the Dumble family – in her letters, Ellen refers to her old school friend Mrs Dumble, a pupil at another Manchester boarding school to the one Ellen attended. Ellen took on the care of her baby stepson Felix and gave birth to a boy, James, in November 1788.

Plate 1.2

**JAMES SHARPLES JUNIOR**

*James Sharples*

c.1802 | Pastel on grey paper | 23 x 18 cm

Bristol Museums, Courtesy Bristol Culture

# MOVE TO BATH

I n 1790, when James was two, the family moved to the Bath area, where they lived at Catherine Lodge, in St Catherine's Valley (Fig. 1). Ellen revelled in the beauty of the natural world here:

> At Batheaston stood some time observing the waterfall and scenery, walked round the mill, and by the side of the river above the fall, the water there as smooth as glass reflected the trees on the opposite side very distinctly, every bough, every tinge of colouring, and the blue sky with the light fleecy clouds gently moving ... On our return listened to the dashing of water, loud cawing of rooks, at intervals the sweet song of birds, at still greater intervals the baying of lambs and the cackling of geese, a curious concert ... saw with pleasure the progress of spring; daisies and yellow flowers now begin to cover the fields, primroses adorn the banks and the violets peep in the hedges, buds of the hawthorn are opening, leaves of the wild roses protruding and the honeysuckle and elders are out in leaf ... it appears to me that a taste for these simple pleasures conduces much to happiness, that they subject us to fewer disappointments and never cause any painful reflections or regret.

Fig. 1
*Catherine Lodge*
Near Bath | Sharples home in the early 1790s

Ellen's mother Margaret lived at Catherine Lodge with her daughter's family until her death, in the winter of 1793.

Commissions, however, were scarce in this romantic idyll. James had to be in town to seek clients and so worked from several addresses in Bath, eventually buying a house at Lansdown Crescent (number 9), which was then still under construction (Fig. 2). This elegant, curved terrace on the northerly slopes of the city was designed by the architect John Palmer for Charles Spackman, a coach builder turned property developer. It was built by various speculative builders between 1789 and 1793, some of whom were ruined by the bank failures of 1793. Spackman in turn was bankrupted in 1795 by the building slump. The Sharples family were among the first residents of the Crescent, with uncompleted houses all around them. The economic consequences of the threat of war with France cast a shadow on Ellen's family, and were to have a profound effect on the direction of their lives.

Fashionable visitors thronged the streets of the Georgian spa, and portrait painters vied with each other to capture the countenances of Bath's ever-changing populace. Mr Ralph, 'an artist of very superior merit', was lately arrived in the city; Mr Hay 'continued to take the most perfect likenesses at two, three or four guineas'; Mr Williams undercut him with his small portraits at one guinea each.

Fig. 2
*No. 9 Lansdown Crescent*
Bath | Sharples home in the early 1790s and in 1801–2

Although there was a steady stream of clients, competition was fierce. In December 1790 the *Bath Chronicle* announced:

> *Mr Sharples Portrait painter in oils and Crayons, respectfully acquaints the Nobility and Gentry that he has taken an apartment at Mr Vaseys, adjoining the Pump Room, where specimens of his performances may be seen, or at his house in Lansdown Place.*

In the winter of 1792 James moved his studio again. An advertisement appeared in the *Bath Chronicle* on 6 December amongst those for Medicated Vegetable Water and Trotters Asiatic Tooth Powder: 'Mr James Sharples, Portrait Painter, is removed from his house in Lansdown Place to No. 16 Queen Square.'

Appropriately for James's inventive pursuits this Queen Square address is now the home of the Bath Royal Literary and Scientific Institution. It may have been here that James made his 1792 portrait of the young Robert Southey (M Shed, Bristol Museums). Southey had just been expelled from Westminster school for writing an article attributing the invention of flogging to the Devil. Born in Wine Street in Bristol, he became one of the Romantic poets and was involved in early experiments with nitrous oxide with Humphry Davy at the Pneumatic Institution in Bristol's Dowry Square, Hotwells. Southey wrote to his brother: 'Davy has actually invented a new pleasure, for which language has no name. Oh Tom! I am going for more this evening, it makes one strong and so happy! So gloriously happy!'[8]

As for the pleasures of Bath, as well as the delights of the health-giving waters, attractions included balls, concerts and plays, while the Lansdown Fair was an annual excitement. A contemporary description anticipates a painting which Rolinda was to make many years later of Bristol's St James's Fair:

> *The grandest assemblage of wild Beasts and Birds In all Europe … in a spacious and commodious Field at Bathwick, adjoining the New Buildings: this grand collection consists of two Stupendous Ostriches, male and female, nine feet high each; a Bengal Tyger, a young lioness, a real laughing Hyena, a ravenous Wolf, an African Ram, and twenty other Animals and Birds; also the Royal Heifer, with two heads; a colt of the race kind, foaled with only three legs, and the double jointed IRISH DWARF; who will carry two men that weigh 20 stone each at the same time.*[9]

Ellen and James's only daughter, Rolinda, was born on 3 September 1793. She was baptised at the tiny church of St Catherine on 1 October, where Ellen's mother Margaret had been buried in February; the start of Rolinda's life and the end of her grandmother's are recorded on the same page of the church record. The ending of

Ellen's duty of care for her mother may have been a factor in suggesting a possible way out of their financial difficulties.

Times were hard, and the economic climate was not conducive to the art market. Britain had expelled the French ambassador after the execution of King Louis XVI on 21 January 1793, and on 1 February France retaliated by declaring war on Britain. The period of the Revolutionary and Napoleonic Wars had begun. Fear of invasion stalked the land, house building had completely stopped and no one was buying paintings.

One response to the crisis, particularly among people with progressive ideas, was to look across the Atlantic. For Ellen and James, the idea of a possible solution to their financial predicament in the new country of America must have become increasingly attractive. After the Declaration of Independence in 1776 a new national identity was being formed; portraits of the important people there were in great demand. The American artists Benjamin West and John Singleton Copley had settled in London, and British artists were discovering an emerging market. Ellen and James may have heard of the success of Robert Edge Pine, a leading London portrait artist who had been working in Philadelphia since 1784 and had recently died there.

The spirit and motivation that Ellen and James must have possessed to embark on a voyage to America in 1794 with their small children at this turbulent time cannot be overstated. The American Revolutionary War of the 13 colonies against Great Britain had only ended a decade before. Rumour of Yellow Fever was just one of the potential dangers: 'Kings and Queens tumbled from their thrones: War laying waste to Europe: and the plague depopulating America!'[10]

Making the voyage was a risky enterprise as the seas were a battleground, with both French and British ships subject to capture. Ellen and her husband would have read the account of Captain Murphy, a passenger on the *Charlotte* – bound for Newfoundland from Bristol, with a Captain Yeatman in charge – which described the capture of their ship by a French frigate and their daring defence and retaking of it:

> ... *being in possession of an old sword, the Captain a small axe and Mr Smith a stout stick, we took the deck against the six Frenchmen, and demanded the vessel, or their lives should answer the refusal, and after a parley of broken English and broken French they surrendered prisoners, and the Captain, myself and Mr Smith have brought the vessel safe into Falmouth. We have sent the French crew to prison, but the Lieutenant is still with us, almost inconsolable, and says he shall lose his head on return to France.*[11]

French privateers in the Atlantic were a constant threat to British and American shipping. In common with their adversaries, the French were licensed in wartime to impound enemy ships, including their passengers, and did so with varying degrees of brutality. In the seven years between 1793 and 1800 some 4,344 British ships were lost, with British shipping losses caused by capture exceeding those arising from the perils of the sea.

The anxieties the young Ellen must have felt can only be imagined. Undaunted by the great obstacle of the sea crossing and the difficulty of travelling with baby Rolinda and their two young boys, the couple must have been convinced that this was the only way to reverse their fortunes. They saw a real financial opportunity in collecting a series of portraits to bring back to England to sell. The severity of the economic depression can be seen in the fact that despite the dangers of the sea crossing, all the American ships from Liverpool and Bristol were crowded with families.

## ACROSS THE ATLANTIC TO THE NEW WORLD

When the Sharples family arranged to let their house in Lansdown Crescent and set sail in 1794, Rolinda was just a few months old and James and Felix were aged six and eight respectively. They took with them a canvas in oils of Erasmus Darwin and some of his large family, as an example to show potential patrons.[12] Dr Erasmus Darwin, grandfather of Charles, was an eminent scientist, an atheist and an early proponent of evolution. A physician and slave-trade abolitionist, in 1788 Erasmus had also written a progressive *Plan for the Conduct of Female Education, in Boarding Schools.*[13] A portrait of 'Miss Darwin in oil' was one of the paintings Ellen later bequeathed to the Academy in Bristol.[14] Mrs and Miss Darwin (possibly Susannah Darwin, formerly Wedgwood, and her daughter Marianne – Charles Darwin's mother and sister) were visitors to the Sharples family home in Bath, suggesting that they shared a similar radical perspective.

When the Sharples couple and their children made their first voyage toward America, we know from Ellen's journal that their vessel was an American ship – unnamed, but it may have been the brig *Union* – bound for Philadelphia and Boston. The ship's Master was John Candler, and this description of the *Union*[15] appeared in the *Bath Chronicle*:

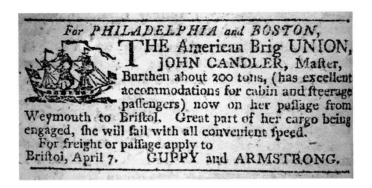

For *PHILADELPHIA* and *BOSTON*,

THE American Brig UNION, JOHN CANDLER, Mafter, Burthen about 200 tons, (has excellent accommodations for cabin and fteerage paffengers) now on her paffage from Weymouth to Briftol. Great part of her cargo being engaged, fhe will fail with all convenient fpeed.

For freight or paffage apply to

Briftol, April 7.        GUPPY and ARMSTRONG.

A few miles off the English coast their worst fears were realised: the brig was seized by a French privateer and all the passengers were taken prisoner and thrown into jail at Brest, where they languished for seven months. A newspaper report relates the likely turn of events:

> *Last week, A French cutter of 20 guns took off the Lands End three brigs, and*
> *after an exchange of prisoners stood away to the southward: one of the brigs*
> *is the Lord Hood of Penzance, laden with wine, the other belonged to Bristol.*
> *The cutter is one of the largest size, sails very fast, and her mast rakes very*
> *much aft: she cruises close to the Lands End.[16]*

Ellen must have needed every ounce of her strength and resourcefulness to manage this situation, caring for her three small children, one a babe in arms, in such squalid and frightening conditions. After the event she found it too unbearable to recollect in her journal, but reflected in general terms:

> *War! How dreadful the sound, whichever way contemplated misery precedes,*
> *accompanies and follows in its train. Our family have experienced, severely*
> *experienced, much of its misery and much did we witness during our seven*
> *months captivity in France, too heart rending to recall.*

The sight of the French bourgeoisie, in desperate straits having lost everything they owned, had a great effect on Ellen. She became determined to find a way to become economically independent and to make her art pay.

On board the ill-fated brig were two other women with young families with whom Ellen developed close bonds during these grim seven months in captivity. One was a Mrs Morgan, who became the subject of a miniature on ivory which Ellen painted some years later (see Plate 3.1). The other was a family by the name of Russell, referred to in the diary of William Dunlap, an American theatre manager who became a friend in New York.[17]

The Sharples family finally arrived in Philadelphia in 1795 and set about establishing a portrait-painting practice. Soon after their arrival baby Rolinda's life was nearly lost when they were involved in an accident in a public coach. William Dunlap recorded an eyewitness account of their journey to Middletown in Connecticut in a stagecoach:

> ... it was midday and in summer, stopped at the inn door to enquire for my friends of the Alsopp family, soon saw the stage, with the horses at full run and no driver, pass me with the rapidity of lightning, the little girl alone in the carriage. On dashed the frightened horses with their light load, and she perhaps unconscious of her danger, soon deviating from the road they struck the carriage against a post, overturned it with an awful crash and leaving it pursued their race. All within sight of the accident ran to the spot with the distracted father and mother, looking to draw from the ruin the lacerated corpse of the child: when on taking out the little creature she was found perfectly unhurt.

After Rolinda's miraculous survival they abandoned public transport. James drew on his scientific skills and constructed a large four-wheeled carriage to contain the whole family, together with all their drawing materials.

Many of the portraits by James and Ellen that are today at Independence Hall (now located in Independence National Historical Park) in Philadelphia date from 1795–7. In 1797 'James Sharpless portrait painter' is listed in Philadelphia's directory as living at 164 South Front Street. This was the family's base for their first two years in America; as their reputation grew they followed commissions, later settling in New York. Crossing the Atlantic an extra 's' was added to the name, and James was known as Sharpless throughout his time in America.

Philadelphia, Pennsylvania was then the capital city of America, having survived a yellow fever epidemic in 1793 which had killed 5,000 of its 50,000 inhabitants. George Washington was into his second term as the first president and lived there until 1796; John Adams, the second president, lived there until 1800. Everyone of political or artistic significance in the US either lived there or passed through the 'city of brotherly love', founded by the English Quaker William Penn in 1682. Penn's experience of religious persecution in England had led him to found the colony that bears his name, a place where anyone could worship freely. Ellen may have wondered at the contradictions in the Land of Liberty: although Pennsylvania had been the first state to abolish slavery in 1780, it was still common. Most of the early presidents and some of James's portrait subjects would have kept slaves.

# EARLY DAYS IN AMERICA

The new artistic life of the Sharples family, so long deferred, now became a reality. James was unknown, and the competition with several British, American and European artists was stiff. The prolific American artist Charles Willson Peale had worked in Philadelphia since 1776; his subjects were the heroes of the Revolution, and he painted George Washington over sixty times.[18] Charles de Saint-Mémin was a French engraver working in profile portraits, while the Scottish brothers Archibald and Alexander Robertson had come three years earlier, establishing the first art school in New York in the 1790s, the Columbian Academy of Painting. William Russell Birch had arrived with his enamel-portrait practice in 1794. John Trumbull, an American artist trained in London and Paris, was making oil portraits of American revolutionary figures.

James had worked in oils as well as pastel in England, but his work in America was exclusively in pastel – or crayon, as it was then called, referring at that time to pigment in a chalk medium.[19] These small, readymade sticks of opaque dry colour, which had been used in a limited form since 1660, were now becoming increasingly available to purchase from commercial crayon makers. Pastel portraits had been popular in Europe in the eighteenth century, following the success of the intimate portraits of the Venetian artist Rosalba Carriera. The naturalism and brilliant light effects of the medium had been dazzlingly demonstrated in the work of several female artists – Elisabeth-Louise Vigée Le Brun, Adélaïde Labille-Guiard and her pupil Marie-Gabrielle Capet – but interest in the medium was beginning to fade.[20] However, accomplished pastellists were something of a rarity in America, and this decision was crucial to the Sharples couple's success.

The advantages of pastel were many. Compared to oils it was possible to make a small portrait in a much shorter time and at a lower cost, and there was a lot less equipment to transport around America. There was no drying time to consider, the colours did not yellow, there was no varnishing or offensive fumes and fewer sittings were required. Essentially, productivity could be greatly increased.

William Dunlap wrote of James:

> He visited all the cities and towns of the United States, carrying letters to persons distinguished, either military, civil, or literary, with a request to paint their portrait for his collection. This being granted, and the portrait finished in about two hours, the likeness generally induced an order for a copy, and brought as sitters all who saw it. His price for the profile was $15; and for the full face $20.

*He painted immense numbers, and most of them very valuable, for*
*characteristic portraiture. His headquarters was New York, and he generally*
*travelled in a four wheeled carriage of his own contrivance, which carried*
*the whole family and all his implements, and was drawn by one large horse.*
*He was a plain, well disposed man, and accumulated property by honest*
*industry, and uncommon facility with his materials.*

James used a greyish brown paper of a slightly rough texture, around seven inches by nine (18 x 23 cm) in size, and always carried a simple gilded-wood frame containing glass; the latter would have been essential to protect the fragile finished surface. He applied the pigment with a brush – 'his colored crayons, which he kept finely powdered in small glass cups, were applied with a camel's hair pencil'[21] – and blended colours with a finger or a tool called a stump. It is likely that he used a measuring instrument called a physiognotrace, which used light to cast a lifesize shadow of the sitter's profile, or a pantograph, a jointed copying frame with which James could have made a scaled reduction of the tracing of the profile.[22] This would certainly fit with James's interest in invention. By comparison Thomas Sully, a nineteenth-century American oil portraitist, took two months to make a portrait and charged $70 for it. James had hit on a cost-effective alternative to the large-scale oil portraits of the growing Federal portrait industry.

## ELLEN JOINS THE FAMILY BUSINESS

Ellen, aware of the demand, was determined to supplement the family's income by using her own considerable artistic skill to make copies of James's portraits herself:

*The continual fluctuation of the funds and other property in which our money*
*had been invested, the uncertainty in mechanical pursuits in which Mr S.*
*delighted: all had an influence in deciding me, soon after our arrival in*
*Philadelphia where Congress then assembled, to make my drawing, which had*
*been learnt and practised as an ornamental art for amusement, available to a*
*useful purpose.*

She started to keep a visual record of every one of James's portrait subjects in case another copy was ever required; her album eventually included 72 closely observed pencil studies – for example, that of the Duc de Liancourt (Plate 1.3), who led a fascinating, well-travelled life, and may even have provided material for Ellen's imagery of a Native American chief (see Plate 2.1).[23] This training was to prove critical to her development as an artist in her own right.

Plate 1.3

**ELLEN SHARPLES**

*Duc de Liancourt*

1803 | Pencil on paper | 84 x 66 mm

Bristol Museums, Courtesy Bristol Culture

Ellen's work soon became indistinguishable from James's, at first adding finishing touches to his pictures, but increasingly producing pieces that were entirely her own. They did not sign their portraits and their styles are difficult to differentiate. Their portraits were 'sturdily honest', the details so accurate that 'on the shoulder the dust from powdered hair … and in one portrait … a scar on the cheek conscientiously reproduced'.[24] Ellen succeeded in turning what was then seen as a lady's accomplishment into a profession, and in doing so she became only the second female artist in America after Henrietta Johnston (b. c.1674, fl. 1705–29), also a pastellist. Henrietta had been active in the southern states; like Ellen her portrait work had developed out of economic necessity and was similarly critical to her family's survival.

In her journal, Ellen said of her work:

> Mr S. was generally engaged drawing in crayons the portraits of the most distinguished Americans, foreign ministers, and other distinguished visitants from Europe. Copies were frequently required, these I undertook and was so far successful as to have as many commissions as I could execute, they were thought equal to the originals, price the same: we lived in good style associating in the first society.

A pastel by Ellen of her fellow countryman, the scientist and theologian Joseph Priestley (National Portrait Gallery, London), from around 1796/7, was probably a copy and one of her first copy portraits. Priestley was in Pennsylvania shortly after being forced to flee England due to his unorthodox religious writings and his support for the French and American Revolutions.

In addition to her portrait work Ellen was also doing some teaching. In a letter dated 28 November 1796 Mrs James Hillhouse wrote to her daughter Mary Lucas Hillhouse, who was staying with the Sharples family in Philadelphia, where Ellen

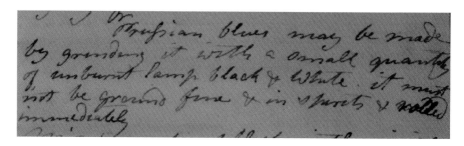

EXCERPT FROM ELLEN SHARPLES'S NOTEBOOK  Prussian blues may be made by grinding it with a small quantity of unburnt lamp black and White. It must not be ground fine and in spirits and rolled immediately.

was instructing her in drawing and French. Mrs Hillhouse lovingly admonishes her daughter as to her manners and choice of clothes, and says: 'always consult Mrs Sharples ... best regard to the Papa and Mama and love to the children. Kiss Rolinda for me. I hope you are very kind and tender to her.'[25]

In 1797 James succeeded in obtaining an audience with George Washington, and another with his wife Martha. This was to set the seal on James and Ellen's success, as they sold many copies of the Washington portrait. On the reverse of the portrait now in the National Portrait Gallery in Washington, Washington's step-granddaughter Eliza Parke Custis inscribed this:

> *This is an Original Portrait of Genl Washington taken in 1797 – it was painted by Mr Sharpless & is an exact likeness except the complexion, Genl Washington was very fair with light brown almost auburn hair – He had not a black beard. He had artificial teeth but so well fixed, that they did not disfigure his mouth – His hair was thin, craped & dress[ed] with powder & pomatum as this profile.*

George Washington Parke Custis, Washington's adopted son, recalled the James Sharples portrait as 'an admirable likeness, the profile taken by an instrument and critically correct'.[26] James's profile portrait of George Washington was considered such a good likeness that it was used as the basis for a postage stamp.

To name just a few of the eminent people who became Sharples portrait subjects: founding father of the USA, Alexander Hamilton (1755–1804), whose family thought it the best likeness of him ever done;[27] Aaron Burr, Vice President (1801–5) under Jefferson, who shortly after the portrait was made killed Hamilton in a duel in Greenwich Village; second president (1797–1801) John Adams and his wife Abigail; third president (1801–9) Thomas Jefferson; fourth president James Madison (1809–17) and his wife Dolley Madison; fifth president (1817–25) James Monroe; Secretary of the US Treasury (1801–13) Albert Gallatin; and Napoleon's chief diplomat Talleyrand.

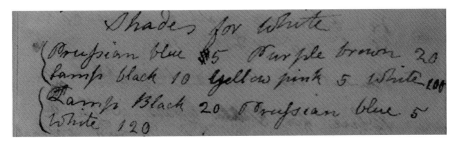

EXCERPT FROM ELLEN SHARPLES'S NOTEBOOK

A letter from a Judge William Cushing of Philadelphia to his niece Miss Esther Parsons, written on 19 January 1797, gives us something of the flavour of the portrait experience:

> *And I must give you a hint, that Mr Sharples from New York has been here some weeks, taking portraits; lodges in the same house with us, and that last week, he took your aunt, and whether you will believe it or not, has given her a prodigious handsome face, and yet, through the embellishments, one may see some of the original lineaments. Also, not liking my portrait taken by him, which I believe you have seen at your uncle George's, he has taken one again, yesterday, which I like much better, though he does not incline to abate much if anything, in the nose.*[28]

Always on the move, in 1797 they were based in New York, during 1798 staying at 272 Greenwich Street, and in 1799 at Upper Reade Street.[29] Entries from William Dunlap's diary evoke their social life:

> 2 OCTOBER 1797 *Afternoon walked out to Sharpless, he has finished a portrait of Mitchill, unlike; begun one of E.H. Smith and wishes to paint one of me. Smith's is very like.*

> 3 OCTOBER 1797 *Afternoon walk with Smith out to Sharplesses.*

> 13 JANUARY 1798 *I met the Club at Smith's, where was Dr Maize of Philadelphia, a pompous young man, Dr Miller, Mr Kent, William Johnson and Mr Sharpless.*

> 10 MAY 1798 *Mr Sharpless called and we settled that Monday should be the day for an expedition to Haerlaam, the party – Smith, Johnson, Miller, Mitchill, Sharpless and wife, Miss Johnson, my wife, myself and Mr Mason an English botanist.*

> 11 MAY 1798 *Sharpless and wife, Mr and Mrs Rogers to drink tea with us.*

> 17 JUNE 1798 *Evening at the Sharplesses. Sharpless and his family were prisoners of the French at the same time that Mr Russell was, with whom I dined at Middletown. S. gives a different portrait of him from what I saw in the drawing room and at table. S. gave a humorous description of a scene he witnessed in a Methodist chapel in his neighbourhood.*

EXCERPT FROM ELLEN SHARPLES'S NOTEBOOK  Mix your Lamp black with spirits and water and ram it into a crucible and burn it until it is almost red hot. It must not be put in too thin.

The Sharples family's first excursion to America had lasted six years and had been an enormous success. In 1801 news reached them that there were problems back home in Bath with the tenancy of their house in Lansdown Crescent, which had remained empty for some time 'in consequence of great injury having been done by the occupants, nailing up pictures on the stuccoed walls &c'.

The political situation was worsening, with a war between France and America threatening. Having done so well with their first venture it seemed a good time to return home to settle their affairs.

Plate 2.1

**ELLEN SHARPLES**

*A Native North American Man*

c.1808 | Watercolour on ivory | 11.5 x 8 cm

Bristol Museums, Courtesy Bristol Culture

CHAPTER TWO

# Bath, Bristol and Back
# to America, 1801–9

O N THEIR RETURN to England, the Sharples found 9 Lansdown Crescent
in a bad state. While they were in America a Mr Sanders – an artist and
drawing teacher – had advertised from their address; no doubt he was the
tenant who had made so many holes in the walls. The family stayed on there for
eight months, making repairs while they looked for somewhere else to live.

James soon left for London to find skilled model-makers for his inventions,
which continued to absorb him, and to undertake commissions. On 10 November
1801 he called on William Godwin, the founder of 'Philosophical Anarchism'. On
the 16th, Godwin wrote in his diary that in between reading Chaucer and Petrarch
and a visit to the Drury Lane theatre he sat for his portrait (James Sharples's
*William Godwin*, Bristol Museums). Godwin was the widower of the feminist writer
Mary Wollstonecraft, who had died four years earlier giving birth to their daughter
Mary, later Mary Shelley.

It may have been on one of these visits that James came across another of his
portrait subjects: John Stewart (Bristol Museums, undated), also known as 'Walking Stewart', who spent his time in the coffee-houses of Piccadilly and meditated in
St James's Park. An influence on Wordsworth and the Romantics, he was a philoso-
pher who had worked as a clerk for the East India Company before travelling alone
through Persia, Arabia and Africa on foot. A vegetarian, he never carried weapons
and was occasionally kidnapped.

One day the Sharples family walked out to their old house in St Catherine's
Valley over Charmy Down, searching for fossils as they climbed the steep hill.
They visited St Catherine's churchyard, where Ellen's mother was buried, and
Ellen remarked on the height of the trees they had planted by their house 11 years
before, remembering their leaving of it:

> admired the house, thought that nothing could be more picturesque or
> the garden in which it was situated; recalled past times and pleasures,
> not without sensations of sorrow and regret, at having left this peaceful abode,
> the consequences of which had been so extremely disastrous.

Before they left Lansdown for a new home, their collection of American portraits was prepared for public view. An advertisement appeared in the *Bath Chronicle* on 13 May 1802:

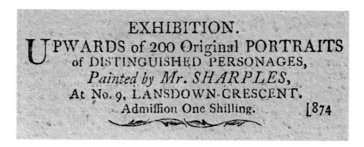

Ellen was happy to be home after their years of travelling:

> *I had once more become attached to Bath and was much grieved at the thought of leaving it. Mr S. said if I so much wished to remain, another house could soon be purchased. We went in search and speedily decided upon No.2 Grosvenor Place, an excellent house commanding varied and beautiful scenery, the price comparatively low in consequence of unfinished houses on each side …*

In January 1803 they moved into Grosvenor Place (Fig. 3). A mile from the centre of Bath, it was part of a terrace designed by John Eveleigh in 1791, as advertised in the *Bath Chronicle*:

> *Grosvenor Place is a very healthy spot and commands very beautiful views of the hills and vales opposite the back part of the house, and of the Kennet and Avon canal, Grosvenor and Sidney [now Sydney] Gardens. The house is at a proper distance from the London and Gloucester turnpike roads.*

On 16 February, Ellen wrote: 'Resumed my drawing, copying distinguished characters in Mr S.'s collection – reduced size in pencil.' They took out a subscription to Grosvenor Gardens – pleasure gardens through which the river Avon flowed – visiting almost every day to 'listen to the nightingales, [and] observe the swift motion of the swallows'.

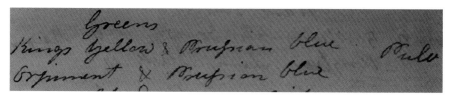

EXCERPT FROM ELLEN SHARPLES'S NOTEBOOK

Fig. 3
*No. 2 Grosvenor Place*
Bath | Sharples home
1803–6

## EDUCATING ROLINDA

Much of Ellen's time was now taken up with nine-year-old Rolinda's education. As an insatiably self-educating woman herself, she gave her daughter an ambitious curriculum, at the end of each year noting an extensive list of her own reading. This included classical and contemporary titles such as: Homer and Cicero (in Latin); John Locke's *An Essay concerning Human Understanding* (1689); Erasmus Darwin's *The Botanic Garden* (1793); William Godwin's *An Enquiry concerning Political Justice* (1793); Joseph-Alexandre Pierre de Ségur's *Women: Their Condition and Influence in Society* (1803); and *A Biographical Dictionary of the Celebrated Women of Every Age and Country* (1804), by the poet Matilda Betham.

'Drawing, reading and instructing my dear Rolinda continues greatly to interest me, as they have done for many years', Ellen observed. There was, however, some gender divide in the subjects that each parent taught: 'Mr S. delights to instruct her in arithmetic and natural philosophy … I attend to her reading, writing, drawing, geography, French etc.' Rolinda was an eager student:

> … leaving off as pleased with the books she reads, the studies she pursues, as with her ball, battle door, [sic; the racket game, battledore] skipping rope and numerous other games, she always returns to them again without the smallest inconvenience.

Ellen was equally concerned with Rolinda's physical development:

> After application for a time to our studies it is a great amusement to me to teach her steps in dancing, and equally amusing to her to imitate them. The active should always alternate with the sedentary.

James Junior and Felix do get occasional mentions in her journal but it is clear who occupied most of Ellen's attention. She suggested that Rolinda should make drawings to illustrate stories in books, but after producing fifty small drawings of Romulus and Remus, her brother James then did the same much better; Rolinda found this humiliating and gave up. The three did have fun together, though: 'Rolinda exceedingly entertained reading with her brothers James and Felix the play of Julius Caesar and catching different characters.'

Both Felix and James excelled at drawing and were already pursuing their own careers as portrait artists. Ellen considered James the finer artist, 'displaying great genius in a boy 14 years of age'. Aged 17, Felix was boarding in Bristol and bringing home books such as Alexander Pope's *Letters*; one day he 'brought home our small one horse phaeton made at New York to a new plan of Mr S.'s contrivance, and which since our return to England had remained in Bristol' (presumably shipped in pieces and then reconstructed).

Meanwhile, Ellen's husband was still occupied with his inventions. On Tuesday, 17 May 1803 a notice appeared in London's *Morning Post* of Mr Sharples's specifications regarding implements for measuring distances.

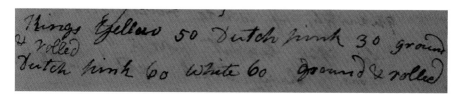

EXCERPT FROM ELLEN SHARPLES'S NOTEBOOK

## ELLEN'S ORIGINAL WORK DEVELOPS

As for Ellen, she was gaining more confidence in her abilities as an artist. She still made copies of James's portraits as an economic necessity, whilst he worked on his contrivances, but from 1803, with the time and space afforded by a more settled existence, she began to think of ideas of her own.

In June 1803 she tried an experiment:

> My first attempt at miniature painting on ivory, copy of Dr Darwin
> [James Sharples, Dr Erasmus Darwin, Bristol Museums, undated].
> Applied every day with attention and pleasure, succeeding better than
> I expected ... Commenced a miniature of Mr S. Should I excel in this style
> of drawing it will be a great satisfaction to me. I shall then consider myself
> independent of the smiles and frowns of fortune, so far as the fluctuating
> and precarious nature of property is concerned.

There was a thriving market for these oval miniature portraits of loved ones or of well-known people – pocket-sized to be held close in the hand, or smaller to be worn on a ribbon on the body or incorporated into jewellery.[1] Ellen began a miniature of Sir Joseph Banks (Bristol Museums, 1803), the botanist who had sailed with Captain Cook on his first expedition. She was pleased with this, and also drew the outlines of Washington and Jefferson as well as making paintings of her two sons.

Overshadowing the Sharples family's tranquillity, however, was the threat of war once more, as Ellen noted: 'The debates in Parliament are interesting but very gloomy, as are all the observations and information in the newspapers. War is inevitable.' This threat was soon to come closer to home and cause great anxiety at Grosvenor Place.

On 18 July 1803, she wrote:

> A printed paper left, [at the Sharples residence] in which was to be marked
> down the number of males and females in the family, what arms we had –
> spades, shovels, saws etc. The males from the age of fifteen to sixty were to
> say in what capacity they would serve in case the French invaded the country,
> whether in the army – act as pioneers – bakers – or supply waggons and horses.

Betty Woodward, an old servant and friend of the family, called from Bristol with news of Felix. Thinking of volunteering, he had asked his mother what she advised, and she in turn had asked Mr S. On not getting a reply, Felix had entered his name. Ellen was alarmed, but after hearing Mr S.'s objections she managed to prevent his enlisting.

In September 1803, shortly after Rolinda's first lesson in Euclid, they rose a little earlier than usual and set off to visit Felix, making the journey to Bristol on foot, as Ellen described:

> … so much pleased with walking that we proceeded all the way, dining at an inn on the road with excellent appetites. On arriving at Bristol we passed through the Fair, amused at the various objects that presented themselves, booths gaily decorated, in front of which men and women in glittering apparel, and fools were exhibiting their anticks to induce the admiring crowd to enter. Drums or fifes, fiddles, organs and tambourines etc at each, playing different tunes which with the various other noises of the fair made a curious concert.
>
> Children on hobbies, in coaches and boats, were whirling round and round – others in coaches ascending aloft and descending. Swings in different places, and of different constructions, all in motion. Everything in the fair animated – buyers and sellers etc.

Ellen recognised Felix's lucky escape from the army:

> The recruiting officer did not fail with drums and colours to entice the raw youth to enlist … Saw Felix and slept at the Montagu … the next day to see the skeleton of the Mammoth, which exceeded our expectations by its prodigious size and form. Afterwards saw a collection of wild beasts and curious birds. The large animals would have appeared much more formidable had we not previously seen the skeleton of the Mammoth, its stupendous size made these seem very small … it was curious to observe the affection the tiger had for a little dog, its constant companion, which he delighted to play with.

The Montague Hotel was at the top of Marlborough Hill at the end of Kingsdown Parade. It was destroyed in WW2 and is now a small green space.

The road home was not so pleasant:

> Engaged places in a coach to return to Bath, set off at one o'clock, our very warm roads extremely dusty, motion of the carriage uneasy, passengers disagreeable, never had so unpleasant a drive, how much preferable to this was walking, very glad to reach home.

One of the few portraits we have of Ellen may date from this time – James Junior made a study of his mother, perhaps in practice for his own career in portraiture. Her clothing is not typical of the period: the red cap looks borrowed from the Renaissance, the ruff collar from the Tudor period (Plate 2.2).

Ellen was now 34 years old. In addition to her concerns regarding the education of Rolinda, her commitment to her own reading, and entertaining callers like

Plate 2.2

**JAMES SHARPLES JUNIOR**

*Mrs Ellen Sharples*

Undated | Pastel on grey paper | 23 x 18.5 cm

Bristol Museums, Courtesy Bristol Culture

Mrs and Miss Darwin, she was ready for a new challenge. Such was the lack of status of female artists at this time that most patrons would not think of employing her, but in October 1803 a commission intended for her 14-year-old son James came her way – Ellen's first original portrait, *Arthur M. Browne* (Bristol Museums). In her words, a certain Miss Serjeant

> introduced her cousin Mr Brown [sic], Prime Serjeant of Ireland, to sit to my son for his portrait. James had just left home for a few days, a great disappointment as Mr B.'s stay in Bath is to be very short. Miss S. prevailed on me to undertake it, and although excessively nervous I succeeded much beyond my expectations. Mrs and Miss S. were highly pleased, pronouncing it an excellent likeness, this was very gratifying to me, who am always timid of my own abilities.

Later that month she continued with her miniature painting of Sir Joseph Banks, and read from Erasmus Darwin's *The Botanic Garden*. One evening the Sharples family entertained a small party of literary gentlemen and discussed whether riches were conducive or essential to happiness.

The end-of-year summary of her achievements that Ellen wrote in her journal included the 58 copies she had made of Mr S.'s originals, plus notes on her extensive reading and on Rolinda's progress:

> Rolinda devoted an hour every morning to geometry and has gone through the first book of Euclid, which with drawing, writing, arithmetic, dancing and walking and working at her little bird (embroidery) … it is delightful to see her always so happy enjoying the present time, free from alarm of the future, which not infrequently disturbs older people that ought with their years to be proportionately wiser.

In early February 1804 Ellen's thoughts also turned to stitching:

> FEB. 1ST *Thinking the Etching of Caius Marius sitting on the Ruins of Carthage [by artist J.H. Mortimer] a good subject for needle work, purchased a piece of white Gros de Naples, framed it, and begun [sic] the outlines.*

> FEB. 2ND *Finished the outlines and commenced the work in which I have been greatly interested … devoting a small portion of time to miniature painting.*

Her skill with the needle had already been demonstrated in America: in the collection at Mount Vernon is a 1797 stitched profile portrait of George Washington.[2] Here she creates subtle modelling with her use of black silk thread on white satin, and the piece reads as a line engraving (*Caius Marius Sitting on the Ruins of Carthage*, Bristol Museums, 1804). Needle paintings, as they were called, were a minor craze in the eighteenth century.[3]

Fine needlework was an essential accomplishment for genteel English women: Queen Charlotte and the ladies at court worked on flower designs provided by the Academician Mary Moser; students in boarding schools embroidered silk copies of book illustrations and prints.[1] Regarded as women's work, historically embroidery had no status in terms of fine art – an aesthetic hierarchy now subject to review.

Rolinda read to Ellen as she sewed:

> *Rolinda reading Madame Genlis – Tales of the Castle whilst I was plying the needle. Rolinda read with uncommon attention the first volume of Homer's Iliad – much interested in the contentions of Agamemnon and Achilles, every line made an impression on her mind. She highly disapproved of the injustice of Agamemnon in demanding of Achilles that he gave up his favourite captive Brisius. Listening to her reading, conversing with her on the subject and others connected with it, engaged the greater part of the morning.*

At the end of March: '… now nearly finished [the Caius Marius piece] and put on a new straining frame, the proper size for the gilded one now making for it'.

Ellen made another minutely detailed stitched picture, *The Fishermen*, that was also taken from a J.H. Mortimer etching, plus two others: *Eastern Heads* and *The Deer Hunt* (all Bristol Museums, dated to early 1800s or dates uncertain).

## A VISIT TO LONDON

James was in London in the spring of 1804 when his older brother Henry died in Liverpool. He sent for Ellen and Rolinda to join him, while Felix was left minding the house with two reliable female servants. Ellen recounts the interminable tedium of a 22-hour journey to London, a number of coaches travelling together for security:

> *At half past 3 o'clock set off in the London coach, each coach holding four, Mr and Mrs Parkins in ours, were pleasant travelling companions with whom we conversed very agreeably for 30 miles and the coach appeared to move rapidly; then our spirits and our conversation began to fail, tea was much wished for, but none could be obtained until we reached Marlborough. How long we are in going, when shall we arrive there? Was often repeated. Entering a town our spirits revived, expecting every moment the coach would stop but on it drove. A turnpike next excited a little hope, an indication of its near approach, and at length to our joy the coach stopped – to our disappointment only to change horses – no refreshments – all the family had gone to bed.*

Resigned to the lack of tea, they tried to sleep.

> *... the sight of Marlborough when we reached it at two o'clock in the morning*
> *gave us very little pleasure, neither did bad tea and supper. Again seated in the*
> *coach a dull kind of conversation was commenced, our sensations not the most*
> *pleasing, neither asleep or awake. Long and wearisome appeared the distance.*
> *We complained of the slow motion of the horses, the pernicious custom of dram*
> *drinking, which occasionally detained the coachman.*
>
> *At 10 miles distance from London the frequency of houses amused us a*
> *little, at 6 miles so contiguous seemed a continuation of town, the frequent*
> *stopping of the coachman put us quite out of patience.*
>
> *At length we reached Piccadilly, observed the elegant houses opposite*
> *St James's Park, the length and spaciousness of the streets we passed through,*
> *but thought we never should get to the end of our journey. The coach stopped*
> *successively whilst different passengers alighted.*
>
> *Near Holborn got into a hackney coach, and reached Furnival's Inn Coffee*
> *House as the clock struck one: there Mr S. always resided in London when*
> *alone. He was out. Ate our breakfasts with excellent appetites.*

So impressed was James by Ellen's recent work in miniature that he passed on a commission for a portrait of Mr Browne's mother. Buoyed up by the positive reception of her recent work,

> *with infinite pleasure I commenced it immediately, applying with steady*
> *attention exerting the best of my abilities. Greatly was I rejoiced on its being*
> *highly approved of ... I also drew three originals in crayons, Miss Austin,*
> *Mr and Mrs Clark, and copied Mr and Mrs B. for our collection, almost every*
> *morning thus engaged during our stay in London.*

They were in London on 1 May 1804 when Ellen was thrilled by the traditional procession of chimney sweeps:

> *decorated with flowers and tinsel and all the colours of the rainbow, dancing to*
> *the sound of a drum and fifes, beating time with their little shovels, so happy*
> *on this day of liberty. One of them had composed of boughs, leaves and flowers,*
> *something in the form of a beehive, large enough to completely cover him.*
> *Thus concealed he walked and danced along the streets to the great diversion*
> *of numerous spectators.*

Rolinda was delighted by the sights and sounds of her first visit to London: the British Museum, St Paul's, the spectacle of thousands of red-coated soldiers drilling in Hyde Park and a performance of Sheridan's *The Rivals* at Drury Lane theatre. A pianoforte was rented for Rolinda's first lessons in 'musick', while their rooms at Duke Street provided entertainment of a different sort:

> *the gentleman of the house of an outrageous temper, was ever when at home*
> *quarrelling with his wife who seemed a meek and good kind of woman.*
> *One day a dish of steaks not being done precisely according to his taste,*
> *he took up the dish with its savoury contents, and the door being open hurled*
> *it into the passage, where against the wall it was broken into fragments …*

Ellen concluded: 'Such doings in the parlour below were quite alarming.'

They subsequently moved to quieter lodgings in Charlotte Street, where they found the silence after Duke Street quite delightful, the only disturbance being the melodious songs of the birds.

## RETURN TO BATH

On their return to Bath, Ellen was shocked by news from America of the tragic death of one of the Sharples couple's most famous portrait subjects, Alexander Hamilton; Bristol Museums holds a fine undated miniature on ivory by Ellen. One of the key figures of early American history, First Treasury Secretary of the United States and the father of seven children, Hamilton had been shot by another of their portrait subjects: his rival, Aaron Burr (portrait of Burr by James Sharples Snr, and pencil copy by Ellen, both Bristol Museums, *c.*1796?).

Ellen wrote:

> *was much affected lately on hearing of the melancholy death of General*
> *Hamilton, the circumstances preceding and accompanying the fatal duel*
> *between him and Colonel Burr; the sorrow manifested by the Americans for the*
> *loss of a man so sincerely and deservedly beloved. This event has made so deep*
> *an impression on my mind, that a succession of images connected with it keep*
> *spontaneously rising and chase away all other thoughts.*

Another of the couple's subjects, Napoleon's chief diplomat Talleyrand (James: *Charles-Maurice de Talleyrand-Périgord*, Ellen: *Prince Talleyrand*; Bristol Museums, both *c.*1796?), possessed a Sharples portrait of Hamilton which he reluctantly instructed his secretary to give to Hamilton's grieving widow, 'notwithstanding the great value Mr Talleyrand sets to the image of a friend of whom we speak every day'.[5]

In December 1804 Ellen records making a copy in miniature on ivory of her husband's portrait of Joseph Priestley (both works: Bristol Museums), the discoverer of oxygen (though another discovered it independently) and a key influence on Unitarianism. She had made an earlier version around 1796/7 in Philadelphia, where Priestley had arrived two years before the Sharples family, after his house in Birmingham had been burned down by opponents of his liberal values. He had seemed a lonely man, soon after losing his wife and son, and was later befriended by Jefferson and Benjamin Franklin.

James's interest in invention led him to seek out the leading scientists of the day for his portrait subjects, some of whom he may have known through his friendship with Erasmus Darwin. The young Humphry Davy, inventor of an early safety lamp, was living in Clifton, Bristol, working as a lab assistant to Dr Thomas Beddoes at his Pneumatic Institution at Bristol's Dowry Square, Hotwells; a fellow lab assistant at the Institution was Peter Roget, who later wrote the *Thesaurus* (James's portraits of Davy and Beddoes: Bristol Museums). Patients suffering from consumption, asthma and other respiratory diseases were offered free treatment at the Institution; as an active member of the scientific community, we might speculate whether James may have participated in some of their more enjoyable experiments with nitrous oxide (laughing gas). Dr Beddoes, a leading figure in the scientific life of Bristol, was also a philanthropist and a political radical. From 1793 until 1799 he worked on finding a treatment for tuberculosis at his clinic in the city's Hope Square. Sadly he died as the result of experiments he tried out on himself. The astronomer William Herschel and the inventor and engineer William Strutt were both James's subjects (Bristol Museums).

## ROLINDA DECIDES TO BECOME AN ARTIST

Felix at 19 and James Junior at 17 were both doing so well at their own portrait work that they were virtually independent. In 1806, on reaching the age of 13, Rolinda decided to follow her inevitable destiny; as Ellen explains:

> [Rolinda] drew the portrait of a young lady of her acquaintance in crayons, which was greatly admired for the correctness of the likeness, and which decided her becoming a professional artist. The praises bestowed on her performances, with the small gold pieces in exchange, were very exhilarating and made her apply with delighted interest, improving rapidly.

Ellen always tried to make education fun. She relates in January 1806 giving Rolinda and her friends two lectures in geography and astronomy, with visual aids, followed by refreshments and dancing. Her efforts with her own work were rewarded as her confidence grew in making portraits from life:

> *Although exceedingly nervous, as I always am when undertaking an original picture, I succeeded in making the likeness of Mr Peart very satisfactory to his friends. I have also drawn Miss Bate and Miss Green in crayons, and Mrs Green in miniature … Rolinda read with very great pleasure Miss Edgeworth's popular Tales … drew the portrait of Mrs Henderson in crayon.*

James had taken out patents for an improvement of the steam engine – receiving praise from James Watt himself: 'Mr Watt of Birmingham acknowledged the great improvement of the steam engine for which Mr S. had taken out a patent.' Another patent was for a forerunner of the pedometer, a small instrument for measuring the number of steps when walking. Yet another counted the revolutions of carriage wheels, recording at any time the distance travelled. Occasionally he took a break from his mechanical pursuits to teach his daughter: 'He was much interested in instructing her in mathematics for which she had as decided a taste as for drawing …'

## PLANS FOR A RETURN TO AMERICA

Meanwhile, before Rolinda turned 13 in the autumn of 1806, a long anticipated return voyage to America had also been attempted by the Sharples family. In May 1806 they had sold the Grosvenor Place house and put all their belongings in store in Bristol. But once again the voyage did not go as planned. In August, as they sailed from Bristol in the *New York Packet*, they received news that war between England and France had broken out once more. Worse still, their ship hit a rock near the mouth of the river Avon near Shirehampton:

> *… the ship lay so much on one side that it was difficult to cross the deck even with the assistance of the sailors. A boat was instantly in readiness in which we were rowed nigh to the Inn at Lamplighter's Hall. After dinner, with a tellescope [sic] we walked by the side of the river to the stranded ship which we perceived to be considerably injured, the rudder broken etc. The Captain represented the injury to be very trifling, but said that it must go into dock to be repaired.*

A long delay ensued; the family returned to their lodgings in Bristol and hostilities between England and France increased. The funds in which Ellen and James had most of their money invested fell in value. Dreading a recurrence of their experience of 12 years previously, they decided to abandon the voyage. Felix and James Junior longed to be in America again and pleaded with their parents to be allowed to go on alone; after much persuasion they were entrusted to the care of Mr Webb, the Captain. They took with them several of their parents' portraits of eminent Americans to serve as models in their new profession, or to sell if need be. This did in fact help them along in their early days: a record exists of a sale in 1806 of two of Ellen's portraits, of George Washington and Alexander Hamilton, to a Mr Connard of New York. Despite violent autumn gales the young men arrived safely; James took lodgings in New York and Felix went on to Philadelphia.

Meanwhile, Rolinda worked hard at her drawing lessons with her father, and having had the benefit of her mother's intensive training she was a confident young woman – unlike Ellen, who often felt so nervous: 'not so Rolinda, who conversed with a person sitting for a portrait with as much ease as if unemployed and made her sitters equally at ease'.

Reassured that their sons were safely established in America, in 1807 Ellen and James went up to London for a time, staying in Hatton Garden. There six of Ellen's miniatures or pastel portraits, including one of George Washington, were exhibited at the Royal Academy exhibition of 1807.[6] This was Ellen's only recorded public exhibition during her lifetime. (For one of Ellen's several Washington portraits, see Plate 2.3.)

Rolinda continued with her lessons on the pianoforte, and became friends with the two daughters of the American Consul. Letters from America were longed for as the Sharples family followed events intensely, waiting for a good time to resume their voyage. Ellen began her 1808 diary:

> *The reading of newspapers engages a portion of time each day. Political news is eagerly sought: we seem to be playing a great game and one that extremely interests us … The rise and power of Bonaparte is unprecedented and most extraordinary; whether it will yet extend or be abridged no one can anticipate … what will be the result of our differences with America in a peculiar manner agitates us with fear and hope and perplexity …*

She felt the separation from her sons keenly. In July 1808 they returned to Bath, visiting old friends and enjoying it so much that they felt regretful of selling the house at Grosvenor Place. Arriving in Bristol they took on rooms at Mrs Hurd's in Park Street, where they stayed while waiting for the right moment to embark.

Plate 2.3
ELLEN SHARPLES
*George Washington*
1803 | Miniature, watercolour on ivory | 71 x 55 mm
Bristol Museums, Courtesy Bristol Culture

Time passed fruitfully, and Ellen's work in this period includes starting a miniature of a Mr Web and – according to a diary note in January 1808 – also starting
'a copy of the Indian Chief', but she does not name her original source (Plate 2.1).
One of James's rivals in America, the French portrait engraver Charles B.J.F.
de Saint Mémin, had made 15 studies of Plains Native Americans from several
tribes.[7] Thomas Jefferson had invited Plains people to visit Washington between
1804 and 1807, following the acquisition of their lands through the Louisiana
Purchase of 1803, when Napoleon sold off French-occupied territory to fund war
with Britain. Ellen would not have seen these paintings, which are in profile and
quite different in style from her naturalistic treatment.

Ellen's painting of the 'Indian Chief' is one of the earliest portrayals of an indigenous American in European Art, and it conveys the dignified presence of the subject. His clothing has been identified as close to the style of an Iroquoian or Algonquian ally of the British in the eastern Great Lakes region.[8] Holding a flintlock rifle in his right hand and with a tomahawk tucked into his belt, his spectacular silver ear ornaments are in the form of the French cross of Lorraine. Brought to North America by the first French missionaries and distributed to converts, these crosses lost their religious meaning when they became highly prized as trade goods between fur traders and native peoples, the two bars indicating higher value. Like the silver armbands and pendant also seen here, they were signifiers of rank and status.[9] Unusually for Ellen, the figure is set in a landscape, perhaps emphasising the sitter's attachment to his land.

Around this time, Ellen painted a miniature of Mrs Gann, started one of Miss Davis and continued work on the indigenous North American. Diversions included reading Milton's *Paradise Lost* and Miss Edgeworth's *Letters*, and visits to the strawberry gardens in Ashton to drink tea with Mrs Maze's family.

> *The beauty of the country around Bristol induced us to take long walks …*
> *often we rambled amongst the rocks at Clifton, listening to the bands of musick*
> *placed at different distances on the summit of the high rocks – the almost*
> *perpendicular precipices below looking tremendous.*

Ellen was quite transported by the sublime effect of these scenes in twilight. More portraits included miniatures of Mrs Carr, Miss Searls and Mrs Baker, and a few other portraits in crayon. Her reading took in the works of the boy poet Thomas Chatterton.


## ACROSS THE ATLANTIC ONCE MORE

At the end of May 1809, James and Ellen felt the moment had come at last when it was safe to make the voyage. They were torn between embarking on the packet from Falmouth or boarding the brig *Nancy* at Bristol, finally deciding on the latter after being convinced by the excellent character of the Captain; they had to provide their own stores.

> *On the 30th of May Mr S., Rolinda, myself and Mary our servant, came*
> *on board the brig at the new basin, in readiness to go down by the evening*
> *tide. A storm of thunder and hail, just after entering – a bad omen – had we*
> *been superstitious.*

Food for the journey was stowed in the bottom berths: wine, brandy, cider, perry and porter, eggs, butter and groceries. Trunks and boxes slid in all directions; two large hams and four hatboxes were swinging overhead. The gale continued to rise, and after the pilot left the ship at Lundy Island a sail was torn to pieces and blew away. Everyone was sick except Rolinda, while one of the hams crashed down and smashed Ellen's straw hat. Ellen describes the harrowing experience:

> The sailors aloft were making horrid noises, sea roared dreadfully … Every
> moment I expected we should be on shore: the violent shocks of the waves
> on the sides of the ship made me often imagine it had struck. Unwilling to
> communicate my fears to Rolinda and Mary I lay awake the whole of the night
> endeavouring to reconcile myself to our fate. It appeared very doubtful we
> should survive the storm.

A week later they had only reached the Irish coast.

> On July 6th recovered from indisposition but dejected by the continuance of
> contrary gales, rainy weather, brig rolling, shipping a great deal of water.
> A swell of the sea rose against the only window exposed without what
> was termed a dead light, broke the glass and rushed in with violence over
> Mr Watson who was reclining in his berth.

Ellen's bottled gooseberries had gone mouldy and one of the pigs had died, as had some of the ducks and most of the fowl, but the north-east wind was favourable and spirits rose.

Ellen passed the time sewing a silk waistcoat for Mr S. Everyone played whist, and Ellen observed the sea creatures – shoals of porpoises and whales seen at a distance spouting up water. The cook nearly caught a shark but it escaped. Mr S. shot a bird called a Mother Cary's chicken, with the Captain rowing out to retrieve it and Mr S. making a drawing of it.

At last, on 21 July, Staten Island came into view, and Ellen breathed a sigh of relief:

> … to be near the shore after a long sea voyage is productive of very pleasurable
> sensations, all agitation and apprehension of danger long experienced suddenly
> ceases, and the mind reposes in tranquillity. It seems like the awakening from
> an uneasy dream.

They had arrived in America for the second time after seven weeks on the Atlantic.

Plate 3.1

**ELLEN SHARPLES**

*Mrs Morgan*

Undated | Miniature, watercolour on ivory | 73 x 55 mm

Bristol Museums, Courtesy Bristol Culture

## CHAPTER THREE

# Second American Visit and James's Death, 1809–11

WHEN THE *NANCY* pulled into New York in July 1809, Ellen was disappointed not to find her son James on the quayside to greet them – he had left for Albany a month earlier. A thriving city on a route popular with migrants, Albany had become the capital of the state of New York in 1797 and was a good marketplace for portrait work. Mr S. engaged apartments at Mrs Williams's, where James had boarded for three years, and the Mr Connard to whom James had sold two of their portraits invited them over, greeting them with flowers, wine and plumb cake. Ellen wrote: 'In the evening we walked upon the Battery, the first music we heard was God Save the King, on the pianoforte, at a house in Broadway.' The tune had been used for new American patriotic songs so may not have been quite the welcome Ellen imagined.

Ellen began house-hunting, and both she and James were astonished at the growth of New York since they had left eight years before. They looked at a house to let in State Street, but hesitated at the rent of a thousand dollars. 'We walked to the upper end of the town; never were we more astonished as in viewing the alterations that had taken place – new houses and new streets extended for miles, in one direction as far as Greenwich …' (today's Greenwich Village). An epidemic of yellow fever had broken out in the city, with two cases near their lodgings, so they accepted an invitation to stay with their friends Captain and Mrs O'Bryant at their country house in Greenwich.

Ellen was most anxious to see their son James, so they braved the August heat and bought tickets for the newly invented and very popular steamboat for the 150-mile trip up the Hudson river to Albany: 'the heat during the night intollerable [sic], and with the biting of certain most annoying little beings prevented anyone from closing their eyes'.

James joined them on board at Albany for an emotional reunion:

> *To see him after so long an absence was indeed a great happiness to us, but to*
> *see him, as we thought, not looking so well as when he left home brought tears*
> *to our eyes.*

## OLD FRIENDS AND A LUCRATIVE INVITATION

They learned from a Mr Dexter that Mrs Morgan and her family – with whom they had been imprisoned in Brest 15 years before, after their disastrous first voyage – resided at Albany, and decided to call on her. At first they did not know each other, but on recognition were thrilled to meet once again and dined together the next day. It may have been around this time that Ellen made drawings of her friend for the undated miniature watercolour painting on ivory (Plate 3.1; Bristol Museums also has a pastel portrait of Mrs Morgan by James Sharples).

The dreaded yellow fever had now reached Albany; several hundreds were ill and many had died. On a visit to 'Balls Town Springs' (now Ballston Spa, in Saratoga County, next to Albany County), Ellen, despite forcing down the nauseating spring waters, became extremely ill with what she believed to be cholera. After recovering and visiting Mrs Morgan again, they hastily sailed back to New York on a packet boat, returning to their lodgings with Mrs Williams.

Here Mr S. suffered a heart attack, the first sign of the heart trouble which was to end his life a year and a half later. Ellen nursed him night and day while their son continued searching every street in the upper part of the city for a house to rent. By the end of the month James had recovered and they agreed with a Mr Knap to rent his house at 3 Lispenard Street, now in the Tribeca district of Manhattan, and moved in on 14 September.

Organising the house and framing pictures took up most of October: 'feathers and ticken [ticking] purchased for beds that are to be made at home ... the pianoforte and carpet brought from England', but Ellen still found time to read George Crabbe's poems and Dr Goldsmith's abridged *Roman History*. She engaged an American woman called Phoebe to help Mary, but Mary, perhaps affected by local independent attitudes, had become what Ellen considered to be insolent – she 'picked up her bundle' and walked out on them, only to return the next day entreating forgiveness and promising to be attentive and obliging. On consideration, they pardoned her.

By December the household had resumed its usual routines, with Ellen setting aside a part of each day to work on her copy portraits and 16-year-old Rolinda taking lessons in music and dancing. Ellen's rigorous reading schedule continued with the Roman orator Quintilian, and she reflects on the importance of being able to express oneself and the neglect of this in education, especially of females. Maria Edgeworth's *Tales of Fashionable Life* and the French Revolutionary Madame Roland's *An Appeal to Impartial Posterity* provided further diversion; ever curious, in April 1810 she attended a course of lectures on chemistry.

Various outings around this time included one to a performance of *Macbeth* starring a celebrated English actor, Thomas Abthorpe Cooper. In May 1810 they were invited to stay at Morrisania, the grand house of one of James's patrons, the American statesman Gouverneur Morris (1752–1816, James's portrait of him: Bristol Museums, 1810), writer of the final draft of the American Constitution and Washington's Minister to France in 1792–4.[1] The house was at the junction of the East and the Haerlaam [Harlem] rivers, in what is now the South Bronx area; Ellen was most impressed by their French tableware and stylish interiors. On 2 June a payment of $50 is noted in Mr Morris's account book for portraits of himself and his wife.[2] Clearly James felt able to charge this patron rather above his usual rate of $20 for a full- or three-quarter-face study.

Through the patronage of Mr Morris, James was invited to join a commission of six engineers and surveyors to Niagara, to investigate the possibility of building canals to join the Hudson river to Lake Ontario and Lake Erie. Since this would also be a chance to view the Falls at Niagara, James could not refuse. Each gentleman was to travel in his own carriage, meeting up at various points. James was offered the honour of accompanying the chairman of the commission, Mr Morris, and his wife; this carriage was followed by a second one containing Mr Morris's French cook and other servants, clearly intending to maintain standards of luxury as they travelled through an uncultivated part of the country.

## SUMMER IN NEW YORK, 1810

Felix was in Virginia and still had not come to see his parents. In June James took a steamboat up the Hudson to visit his younger son in Albany, joining Mr Morris's expedition there. Meanwhile, back at home Ellen was preserving raspberries and pineapples, in any spare moments between copying portraits of Mr Morris and of the leading judge, William Paterson. Her assiduous reading included Matilda Betham's *A Biographical Dictionary of the Celebrated Women of Every Age and Country* and Washington Irving's *A History of New York … by Diedrich Knickerbocker*, a satirical work. On 4 July Ellen and Rolinda 'were not much amused' by the Independence Day parade on Broadway:

*a full length portrait of Gen. Washington decorated with festoons of blue silk,*
*a gilded eagle on the top, was placed upright on a kind of bier and carried on*
*the shoulders of a great number of men; this, and a few flags, were all that*
*constituted the show, in honour of the American independence.*

They thought the band indifferent, with the men not marching in time. The firing of cannons shook everything: 'on the way home called on a lady who said her infant, not a fortnight old in his cradle, screamed every time a cannon was fired!' However, as she watched the procession Ellen may have reflected with some gratitude on the enormous debt her family owed to the countenance of this great man, once an officer in the British army. Painted by James and Ellen multiple times, his face had indeed been their fortune.

Ellen was again having trouble with Mary, 'who, being insolent, packed up her garments and set off in my debt. A little girl not far distant came to assist us, whose good nature compensated for her want of skill.' She engaged an American woman, Betsy Jackson, in Mary's place.

Once again Ellen received a commission for an original painting due to a male member of the family being unavailable, as had happened in Bath in 1803 in the absence of her 14-year-old son, James. She was persuaded by a Mr Onderdonck to make a pastel portrait of his brother. Ellen had been taken very ill during the night but demonstrated her professionalism by managing to carry on 'by extreme exertion and prescription of Dr Miller'.

The portrait was completed in three days to the great satisfaction of the gentleman and his friends, whose compliments Ellen found very gratifying, 'as was also recovered health'. She also painted a miniature on ivory of a child, 'Master Radcliff', and copy portraits of Mr 'Griscomb' (the scientist and educator John Griscom) and a Mr Davey. Her reading at the time was Alexandre-Joseph-Pierre Ségur's *Women: Their Condition and Influence in Society*, translated from the French.

On an excursion to the Elgin Botanic Garden (three miles from the city at that time and on the site of the present Rockefeller Center), Ellen met the physician and botanist Dr David Hosack and his wife. David Hosack had created this public botanic garden – America's first – at his own expense. Named after his father's Scottish birthplace, it was home to around 1,500 species of indigenous and exotic plants.

Hosack was also the doctor who had attended Alexander Hamilton after the fatal injuries he sustained in the duel with Aaron Burr. In August 1810, Ellen and Rolinda made a trip to Weyhook (now the 'Weehawken Dueling Grounds') to see a monument to Alexander Hamilton: despite thunderstorms and fighting off swarms of mosquitoes, they rowed in a leaky boat to see the stone tablet commemorating the spot where Hamilton had fallen, now opposite 42nd street on the New Jersey side. Ellen recalled:

> *on retiring to our apartment Rolinda and I spent an hour killing musquitos; leaving a candle burning we then ventured to lie down, but the teasing insects soon made us rise to look about and destroy them; thus went on all night, had no sleep, and in the morning our faces, hands and feet were swollen prodigiously.*

They returned home gratefully 'with most disfigured countenances' from the bites and went straight to sleep.

## AN EXCURSION SOUTH

James returned from Buffalo, with continuing health problems giving him severe pains in his side, and Ellen admired his sketches of the Falls at Niagara. In September they boarded a steamboat to Brunswick to visit Miers Fisher (portrait by James Sharples: Bristol Museums, undated) and his large family at 'Eury' (now Ury), 10 miles from Philadelphia.

Fisher was a Quaker lawyer and slave-trade abolitionist. James and Ellen had become friends of the Fisher family 14 years before, and on this visit accompanied them to the local Friends meeting. Ellen's account of this reads as if the experience was a new one to her, and not as though she were a fellow Friend – underscoring doubts about her suggested Quaker connections. James made portraits of Fisher's daughters, Miss Sally and Miss Lydia, and Rolinda had her first rides on horseback, 'induced to do so by the gentleness of Miss Hanna's pony' – Hanna being another Fisher daughter. Ellen was impressed by these well-educated girls, 'devoid of pride, vanity and selfishness', who were also making articles of clothing for poor families.

In Philadelphia they visited the museum that Charles Willson Peale had established to display his portraits of 'noted worthies', first at his own house, then at the old Pennsylvania State House. Some eighty of these now form the nucleus of the collection of the Portrait Gallery at the Independence National Historical Park.[3] The portraits were presented together with taxidermy, fossils and specimens of natural history, birds and mammals which were – a new idea – displayed in museum cases with painted backgrounds depicting the creatures' natural habitats.[4] These seem to have made more of an impression on the family than the portraits: they saw 'the rattle snake and a canary bird living in the same cage; two camellions [sic] alive, a wild turkey and some immensely large shells'. At their lodgings that night they could not sleep but Rolinda and a young lady played piano duets to distract them from the heat and the odious mosquitoes.

The next day they sailed on the packet for Burlington, New Jersey, with Ellen reading Count Rumford's *Essays* on board, which (rather oddly) contained tips on making 'hasty puddings' and 'cheap soups'. On returning home Ellen thought 'the harbour of New York never appeared more beautiful'.

Finding their son James at home, quietly amusing himself reading, Ellen seemed a little surprised to discover that everything was in order. She praised Betsy's honesty and reflected on how lucky they were to have her. As usual she recorded domestic detail alongside the intellectual: peaches are bought for preserving, and mangoes and cucumbers for pickling. While reading Livy's *History of Rome*, she remarked on how much pleasure reading Latin gave her, despite Rolinda not wishing to learn. In October 1810, James Junior returned to Albany without Ellen to see him off: 'my eye so much swollen with the bite of a musquito prevented my accompanying him to the steamboat'.

## MIXED FORTUNES

The report on the canal project with which James Senior was involved was published and work on it was soon to begin, to be funded by Mr Van Renselaer, one of the commissioners and also one of the richest men in America, whose copy portrait Ellen was currently drawing: 'Mr S. speaks of him as a most amiable and accomplished gentleman.' Mr Jones and Mr Gerrard sat for portraits by Mr. S, whose illness was becoming more apparent as the winter drew on. Ellen was much occupied attending to him and also sewing, which prevented her from drawing and pursuing her studies: 'purchased some Newtown pippens [sic; a very popular US apple at the time] for the winter, laid in a stock of wood and had paper pasted on every crevice in windows'.

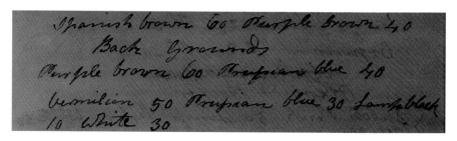

EXCERPT FROM ELLEN SHARPLES'S NOTEBOOK

James's illness was diagnosed as angina pectoris, and through the exceptionally cold winter Ellen became more and more concerned by his weakening condition, only getting out of the house occasionally with Rolinda to attend 'Mr Griscomb's' (John Griscom) lectures on philosophy. James still managed to give his daughter lessons in mathematics, at which she was rapidly improving. Ellen wrote:

> *In a room in which was a blazing fire night and day, Forts Thermometer never rose above 26 … water froze on a table near the fire and on the mantel piece; streets were covered with snow. This intense cold was particularly distressing to Mr S. who, in addition to the complaint of the heart had a dreadful cough. Rolinda in a warm cloak and snow boots, was interested in walking every day a mile or two in search of something that she hoped would be agreeable to her father. James returning from Albany on his father's becoming so ill, accompanied her. Nothing could exceed their affectionate attentions. Our servants most cheerfully aided us in every way they could. Dr Miller is exceedingly attentive.*

James bore his illness with resignation, 'but nothing could be more distressing than to witness his suffering, all hopes of his recovery now withdrawn his release was almost desired'. Their many friends called, offering assistance, but at 6 o'clock on the morning of 26 February 1811 James died. Ellen was heartbroken.

Felix arrived from Virginia just too late to speak with his father. Ellen's friend Mrs O'Bryant arranged the funeral and James was buried at St Peter's Catholic Church in Barclay Street, with some of his numerous friends acting as pall bearers. Ellen reflected:

> MARCH 25TH *This has been a melancholy fortnight spent in painful retrospection and distressing anticipations. When I could apply to business was engaged in preparations for leaving New York. It has been the anxious wish of Mr S. during his illness that in case of his death, I should return with James and Rolinda to England. He was apprehensive that war would break out between the two countries, and that we might experience inconvenience by remaining: the climate he was assured less favourable to health, the loss of which would be ill compensated by pecuniary advantages in the investment of property, and professional success that America certainly possessed.*

He had already transferred the considerable sum of £5,000 to the bank in London in anticipation of their return.

Felix was 'very partial to America and wishes to remain'. James left him £500 and 1,800 acres of land in Pennsylvania, while Ellen gave him their books, drawing materials and many of their portraits of distinguished Americans, introducing him to all their friends and acquaintances in the hope that he would be induced to remain in New York.

# PACKING UP

Ellen prepared for their final departure. The family's household goods were auctioned and Ellen was dismayed at the low price fetched by Rolinda's pianoforte. Despite their grief Ellen and Rolinda found comfort in their art: Ellen was still working stoically at her copy portraits and finished a miniature of a Mr Russell, 'which was highly approved of'. She and Rolinda took ferry rides to Brookline (now Brooklyn) and Hoboken, New Jersey, and Rolinda made a study of tulips from nature 'which was most admirably done'.

Ellen booked their passage to Liverpool on the *Magdalen*, but before embarking they visited the American Academy of the Arts in the former Governor's house, 'which has but lately been established'. They were most impressed by the three large rooms exhibiting pictures and plaster casts: 'Venus, Apollo Belvedere, Castor and Pollux, these as large as life occupy one room in which there is a sky light.' The Academy had been established in 1808 in the upper floors of this Georgian-style building at the end of Broadway, south of Bowling Green. Perhaps Ellen was to remember this experience many years later when she decided to give her legacy to the Bristol Academy for the Promotion of the Fine Arts (now the Royal West of England Academy, or RWA).

Ellen's friends prepared for her departure:

> *Miss Glass presented me with some spices, as she said for the voyage, enclosed was an elegant pin, topaz set in pearls and gold, a pair of lace sleeves for Rolinda and a most kind supplementary note.*

On 29 May Ellen, James and Rolinda set sail, with Felix coming aboard to say adieu. They were never to meet again. Ellen explained: 'He intends to visit Mr Fisher near Philadelphia and make inquiries concerning his lands, I fear will proceed to Virginia, which seems his favourite place of residence.'

Felix became so thoroughly Americanised that only a year later he signed up as a volunteer rifleman with the 61st Regiment of the Virginia Militia to fight against the British, rising to the rank of corporal. He advertised his services as a drawing master in the newspapers of Norfolk, Virginia, and continued to ply the family trade in Virginia for some years – his pastel portraits are in a freer style than those of his parents and are often three-quarter view or full face, in contrast to the in-profile views of his father.[5] A record survives at Bristol Archives of an 1814 debt incurred in Virginia and settled by Ellen's bank, hinting at a somewhat precarious existence. In March 1816 he wrote her a scrawling letter from Baltimore, in answer to hers, which had taken four months to arrive. In it, he said: 'I am obliged to scribble as fast as I can as two gentlemen are waiting in the other room to sit for their pictures.' Addressed to her 'care of Peter Maze Esq., Bristol', he thanks her for money she has sent and claims that he has 'as much to do as he can attend to [producing pieces priced] at $15 without a frame and this business is likely to increase'.

At some point Felix visited Yardley, the estate of the Winder family in Northampton County, Pennsylvania, where he obtained a loan from Levin Winder, leaving the family collection of pastels behind as collateral. He never returned for the pastels, and they were eventually sold by Winder, many of them ending up in the collection at Independence Hall.[6] Felix apparently took to drink and died after an unhappy love affair in around 1830.[7] He is buried at Isleham, the Yeatman family plantation, in Mathews County, Virginia.


## A LAST SEA VOYAGE

On board the *Magdalen,* Captain Sketchley introduced Ellen to the other ladies, and after anchoring overnight near the recently constructed lighthouse at Montauk Point, the pilot left them the next morning, taking with him a farewell letter to Felix. Ellen found leaving New York an emotional experience which 'brought many melancholy retrospections and reflections into my mind'.

Once again all the ladies except Rolinda were seasick.

> JUNE 11TH  *The passengers have been very good humoured … none having habits annoying to the others. The gentlemen are extremely polite to the ladies, none of them smoke or indulge in wine … Rolinda every day sketching one or other of the passengers who are exceedingly amused by her drawings and much extol her talents … a few whales were sporting one day and a few porpoises another. I have amused myself reading Mr Greoves Spiritual Quixotte [Richard Graves's The Spiritual Quixote], an entertaining work; Life of Buonaparte, and occasionally learning Latin in Horace, sewing etc. Rolinda has an inflamed eye, which gives me uneasiness, in other respects she is perfectly well and in excellent spirits.*

> JUNE 16TH  *The weather has changed from cold and rainy to a most agreeable temperature … we are generally upon deck: all are in good spirits … books, cards, backgammon, chess and needlework, engage different groups, while others are walking the decks, or exercising their skill in adroitness, strength or agility.*

But spirits fell as the wind changed, and with it Ellen's respect for the gentlemen's behaviour:

> JUNE 23RD *For two or three days we have been tacking about the Irish Coast making very little progress, the wind being directly contrary. On the 21st a fishing boat came up to us and ten of the passengers concluded to sail in her to Kinsale, proceed by land to Dublin and thence in the packet to Holly Head [sic] and through Wales to Liverpool … We all begin to express uneasiness and impatience at being thus detained … we got a supply of fish from the Irishmen but they had been too long out of their own element.*

> JUNE 24TH *Wind directly contrary and all the passengers wearied out with disappointed expectation, the Captain almost in despair. A few of the gentlemen sat longer over their wine than usual to drive away vexation, the very worst thing to have recourse to in any kind of difficulty or disturbance …*

> JUNE 25TH *The gentlemen who had erred in their judgment yesterday were ill today which greatly aggravated every other disagreeable sensation. Mrs Lonsdale's child was in fits, her death expected every moment, revived twice by immersing her feet in warm water and dropping chicken broth into her mouth. Mrs L. in great agony. Afternoon a calm succeeded the high wind. A boat came from an American ship that was bound from New York, and the Captain and Mr Russell came on board affording me an opportunity of writing a few lines to send to Felix.*

## HOME SHORES

At last, on 29 June 1811 and after four weeks at sea, they reached Liverpool, where they booked into the Star and Garter tavern before engaging apartments on the corner of Duke Street for three weeks. George Sharples, James's eldest son and James Jnr and Rolinda's half brother, also an artist, visited them every day. Ellen made a sentimental journey to Everton to see the house that she and James had lived in when they were first married. They enjoyed the elegance of the public buildings but 'the walking on the round stones and pebbles is exceedingly unpleasant to those who have been accustomed to flagged footways'.

There were visits with George to James's nephew William Sharples and his 'exceedingly friendly family', to the Botanic Garden and to an asylum for the blind which they were much affected by. James Jnr left for Bristol and Ellen and Rolinda travelled to London to the bank, where Ellen had to prove her husband's will; they stayed at their former lodgings in Hatton Garden.

James had left everything to Ellen apart from £200 to George, who had already received his mother's marriage portion, £500 to Felix with his 1,800 acres in Pennsylvania, and £1,000 each to James Jnr and 'my amiable daughter Rolinda'. He appointed

> *my faithful and much respected wife Ellen Sharples sole executrix ... fully confiding that she will act with that fidelity and discretion in respect of the future disposal of the rest of the property with which she has conducted herself through every condition of life.*

Ellen reflected on her lack of experience in matters of business, and this ordeal caused her so much anxiety that her hands shook:

> *Going to the bank, and the Attorneys, caused me a great deal of agitation and when I had my name to write my hand shook so that it was with difficulty I could do it. Girls as well as boys should be accustomed to transact business of various kinds and to enter publick banks and offices which would prevent the distressing sensations which women experience when obliged to do it late in life. Extreme timidity gives awkwardness and disqualifies anyone from acting with perfect propriety. A proper degree of confidence and firmness is of inestimable advantage.*

Ellen sold exchequer bills and purchased Navy 5 per cents (share certificates[8]). George met them and received his legacy. She and Rolinda also purchased a Broadwood pianoforte and arranged for it to be sent to Bristol. They engaged places in the Oxford mail coach service and speedily arrived in Bristol, where they dined at the Bush Inn in Corn Street and engaged lodgings in Queen Square for one week.

Plate 4.1

**ROLINDA SHARPLES**

*Portrait of the Artist*

c.1814 | Oil on panel | 31 x 25 cm

Bristol Museums, Courtesy Bristol Culture

CHAPTER FOUR

# Bristol, London and Recognition for Rolinda, 1811–20s

O N HER RETURN to Bristol in the autumn of 1811, Ellen faced the rest of her life with her two adult children. Many women might have retired gracefully after such adventures – at 42 she would have been considered old, as the average age to which people lived was only around forty at that time. However, the spirit and resourcefulness with which she had fashioned her own dramatic and eventful life did not desert her now.

Ellen's next challenge was to set up her beloved daughter as an artist in her own professional practice. This was an unheard-of ambition for a provincial young woman in England in the second decade of the nineteenth century: it would not have happened without Ellen's determination. Unlike in France, where several male artists had accepted female students, and women professionals were part of the art world, England had few working women artists at this time.[1] It was considered highly unbecoming for a lady of Ellen's class to earn money from her activities, and even worse to draw attention to herself and to seek to make a living from it.[2] Emboldened by the success of her own work in America, Ellen had other ideas.

Her life became focussed on making Rolinda's career a reality, to be cultivated with the utmost decorum and propriety:

> the employments now most interesting to me are those in subservience to my
> dear Rolinda, I am always at her command, to read to, or listen to her reading,
> to accompany her on a walk, amuse her sitters, converse with her visitors, when
> not convenient for her to see them, ornament her dresses, go or come, or in any
> way make myself useful.

One might wonder how much choice Rolinda had in her mother's plans, as she was almost as interested in music as in painting around this stage, an inter-est suggested clearly by Plate 4.1. Certainly Ellen's journal reveals nothing but absolute compliance and devotion to her mother. The family stayed until 1812 at drawing-room apartments – rented accommodation with a large reception room for receiving visitors (including business clients, such as portrait-sitters if you were a Sharples) – in Orchard Street, central Bristol. There was great concern at this time about the quality of the Broadwood piano which had been purchased in London – Rolinda had lessons twice a week with a Mr Bryant and devoted two hours a day to practising. In February 1812 they were thrilled to receive two letters from Felix in Norfolk, Virginia, along with a jar of delicious sweetmeats.

A group of portraits that may be among Rolinda's earliest ones – although they could, in fact, be by her brother James Jnr or by Ellen – are in the family tradition of pastel portraiture. These pastel drawings with watercolour are of three children and were completed between around 1809 and 1815. The children in question are those of Dr John King (Johann Koenig) and Emmeline Edgeworth King: sisters Zoë and Psyche and their brother Edgeworth (one of Zoë, by Rolinda or James, *c*.1811–13; one of Psyche, by Rolinda or James, *c*.1809–11; and three of Edgeworth, one by either Rolinda or Ellen, one by Rolinda or James, and one by James, *c*.1812–13, *c*.1815 and *c*.1814 respectively; all at Bristol Museums). Obviously adored by his family, Edgeworth sadly died in 1817 at the age of 10. Dr John King (whose portrait, by James Jnr, is also in Bristol Museums) was a surgeon and Bristol School artist who worked with the scientists Thomas Beddoes and Humphry Davy. The King and Sharples families became good friends and would be long-standing near-neighbours – the Kings lived in the Mall, Clifton, and the Sharples family were soon to begin an extended period living in Clifton.

In June 1812 Rolinda began to experiment with oils: 'Rolinda commenced oil painting on the 21st and has since applied with great ardour.' That summer they accompanied their friends the Mazes to the strawberry gardens at Ashton. Ellen, ever the assiduous student, was reading Plutarch's *Lives* and a history of Peter the Great as she worked on a dress for Rolinda, 'she much interested in oil painting, music and other studies'.

At the end of the year and the beginning of 1813, Ellen 'sat for my picture to Rolinda in oil colours, large as life, kit kat size, the first portrait she painted in oils'. 'Kit-kat' – usually Kit-cat – size is typically 36 x 28 inches (91.5 x 71 cm), showing a portrait view that is less than half full-length but includes the hands. The term originated in the early eighteenth century when the owner of London's Kit-Cat Club ordered portraits of its members at this size. By taking up oil painting and working at a larger scale, Rolinda was demonstrating her ambition – and breaking with the established tradition of the rest of the family.

# A MOVE TO CLIFTON

On 24 March 1813 the family settled in Clifton, in a part of Clifton now called Clifton Village which was, indeed, then a village quite separate from Bristol, only officially becoming part of the city in 1835. Humphry Davy wrote to his mother of Clifton:

> *commanding a view of Bristol and its neighbourhood, conveniently elevated*
> *above the dirt and noise of the city. Here are houses, rocks, woods, town and*
> *country in one small spot, and just beneath us the sweetly flowing Avon,*
> *so celebrated by the poets.*[3]

Sion Spring House, on Sion Hill, the Clifton home of the Sharples family until 1820 (Fig. 4), was at the top of the cliff known as St Vincent's Rock, high above the river Avon and the Hotwell [Hot Well] (giving the nearby area of Hotwells its name) below – Clifton and surrounds drew large numbers of people who came to take the well's supposedly health-giving waters. Overlooking the Avon Gorge and Leigh Woods, a year's rent for their new home was £90. They took long walks and spent much time at the windows:

Fig. 4
*Sion Spring House*
Clifton | Sharples home 1813–20

*the back drawing room, Rolinda's painting room, looks over the garden,*
*beyond is a large field, in which a walking path by a pretty rural hedge leads*
*into the Mall, the view of the Clifton Hotel and Assembly Rooms.*

A Miss Harriet Pigott, a 'most talented agreeable lady', occupied the other set of drawing-room apartments on the same floor, while two military gentlemen, General Gordon and Captain Stewart, lived in the very large parlour below.

Their usual routines were soon resumed, with Rolinda continuing with her crayon (pastel) portraits, starting work on a portrait of her friend Miss Eliza Cumberland (daughter of George Cumberland, amateur artist, collector and friend of William Blake), while Ellen read to her from Maria Edgeworth's *Letters for Literary Ladies*. Edgeworth's phrase 'all that I dread is that apathy which philosophers call tranquillity' would have resonated with them both.

The Royal Academician Edward Bird (1772–1819) was the only artist with a national reputation in Bristol at that time. A painter of historical and genre scenes, his work showed groups of figures in a contemporary setting, painted in a naturalistic style. Bird was at the centre of an informal group of artists and art lovers which met to talk and drink, and to go on evening expeditions to sketch from nature. This included their friend Dr John King, Francis Danby, Samuel Colman, Samuel Jackson, ironmaster and patron John Gibbons, Nathan Cooper Branwhite and Edward Villiers Rippingille. Other members of the circle were Francis and Henry Gold, the Reverend John Eagles and George Cumberland. This was the genesis of what later became known as the Bristol School. Their inspiration was the landscape around Clifton, in which they saw the epitome of Romanticism – such a dominant theme in early nineteenth-century art and literature:

*Leigh Woods, what memories and associations do they recall, Chatterton,*
*Southey, Coleridge, C.A. Elton and J. Eagles with other congenial spirits,*
*have wandered and mused amid their song inspiring shades, the very land of*
*poetry and enchantment.*[4]

If Ellen had hoped that Rolinda might benefit from the society of these artists she was to be disappointed, as she was excluded from this congenial group by virtue of her gender. Rolinda's art, in fact, was marginalised by her contemporaries for most of her life, and it was not until 1832 that her work received its first acknowledgement at the newly formed Bristol Society of Artists, when one painting by Miss Sharples was exhibited. Mr Jackson showed 13, Mr Danby 5, Mr Rippingille 4. Any association with them would have been considered quite improper, but Edward Bird's genre scenes were to have an influence on the direction of her painting.

Eliza's father George Cumberland did provide Rolinda with some introductions but later wrote:

> *Miss Sharples' pictures – two of them sold at auction to Mr Dance who knows nothing of painting for £50 – she had previously sold them to another simpleton for £150 or thereabouts who broke down afterwards – she has a very tolerable picture of the Broken Bank here for which she expects £150 and says she has been offered £100 by a Liverpool man. I advise her to send it to Hobday as some London Banker may buy it out of spite to Bristol.[5]*

If we look at the subject of one of Francis Danby's best-known works we can appreciate Rolinda's difficulties in her attempts to establish herself as a serious artist. *Disappointed Love* (Victoria and Albert Museum, 1821) shows a distressed young woman of about Rolinda's age in a melancholic pose. A miniature portrait of her lover, together with her shawl and bonnet, lie at her side while torn-up pieces of a letter drift away on the water. This was an archetypal image of a young woman that was prevalent in the culture of the day – decorative, weak and vulnerable.

If Rolinda's work was not receiving the attention it deserved, Ellen was undeterred. James Jnr continued to make small-scale portraits in the family's traditional style: 'the portraits executed by my son James are much admired, he has had many commissions, generally going out to draw'.

## A VISIT TO LONDON AND ITS AFTERMATH

Convinced, however, of her daughter's future beyond that of a provincial artist, Ellen was determined to keep up with artistic developments in the capital. Her account of one visit gives a flavour of the art world at the time.

In May 1813 Ellen, James and Rolinda set off in the night coach for a three-week visit to the capital, lodging with a Mrs Bull not far from Somerset House, where the Royal Academy was located until 1837. They spent six hours viewing paintings at the Royal Exhibition, and saw some of Turner's sea pictures: 'we greatly admired a picture of a storm, finished in a coarse style, but which at a proper distance had a wonderful effect'.

They called at Mr Stothert's (Thomas Stothard, 1755–1834) with a letter of introduction from George Cumberland. Stothard painted groups of figures often based on literary themes and showed Rolinda 'how to make up her palette and some new vehicles to be used in painting'.

At the British Institution they saw paintings by Hogarth, Gainsborough, Wilson, Mengs and Zoffany. At Thomas Brown artists' suppliers in High Holborn they spent much time purchasing canvas, colours, brushes and panels and selecting plaster casts of human anatomy, to be packed up and sent to Clifton. Drawing plaster casts of Greek and Roman sculptures was the primary method of instruction at that time, and the only means of studying the human form for women, as they were not permitted to attend classes to draw from life (thought an unseemly thing for women to do). Days were also spent viewing old masters at the salerooms, with Ellen carefully noting down prices: 'Sir Thomas Lawrence charged 80, 100, 150, 200 and 300 guineas for the different sizes.'

They discovered that the Royal Academician Philip Reinagle (1749–1833), whose animal and landscape paintings they admired, gave lessons at 2 guineas each, and Rolinda was signed up:

> *We spent a whole morning there, and she received instructions that have been highly advantageous to her. Mr R. bestowed uncommon attention, omitting no information that he considered would be useful, employing me the whole time she was practising to write down the instructions according to his dictation – his daughter, a pleasing girl, was copying a landscape.*

**EXCERPT FROM ELLEN SHARPLES'S NOTEBOOK:**
Carmine crayons never to be dried by the fire

Rolinda was to receive 10 more lessons, from Reinagle's son Ramsay, on a later visit in 1820, which consisted of her copying 'a picture of an old master, figure of Aaron holding his rod budding, which Mr R. recommended for effect'. This was the full extent of Rolinda's formal training, apart from her parents' instruction.

That winter of 1813, just after her twentieth birthday and inspired by the London visit, 'Rolinda commenced a second picture of myself, large as life, kit kat size; she, now much improved in painting, having become discontented with the one executed in January.' Conditions were far from perfect; it was an exceptionally harsh winter when frost fairs were held on the frozen Thames: 'Small progress has been made in my portrait, days so very dark and cold … but by a blazing fire Rolinda drew from casts and read … snow several feet deep.' In January 1814: 'Rolinda finished my portrait.'

The painting referred to here could be Rolinda's painting of her mother at afternoon tea, although Ellen's memory may be faulty as this portrait is smaller than kit-cat size (Plate 4.2). Rolinda presents a figure in a relatively active pose –

Plate 4.2

**ROLINDA SHARPLES**

*Portrait of Mrs Ellen Sharples*

c.1814 | Oil on canvas | 31.5 x 25.5 cm

Bristol Museums, Courtesy Bristol Culture

a significant departure from the family style and a prelude to her more ambitious later work. The picture begins to tell a story rather than to simply record the features of the sitter. Ellen, in a lacy cap and ruffled fichu, presides decorously over teacups, a silver teapot and a milk jug on the japanned tray. Perhaps this domestic scene would have been accompanied by a slice of home baking; Ellen thoughtfully left us her recipe book, and her plumb cake was a favourite. Not all the recipes in her book are so wholesome, however: her advice on how 'To Dress a Turtle About Thirty Pounds Weight' is quite gruesome.[6] Ellen was clearly not squeamish; the recipes reflect her practical approach to life.

Not content with music and painting, 'Rolinda takes great delight in chemistry' and 'sometimes entertains us with curious and beautiful chemical experiments'. Ellen obviously took pride in her daughter's achievements:

> It is very delightful for me to see her always cheerful and happy, ardently
> engaged in various intellectual pursuits, particularly that of painting,
> for which she has a decided taste. Exercising it as a profession she views it as
> attended with every kind of advantage. The employment itself is a positive
> pleasure; it procures in exchange many articles of utility and luxury that
> otherwise would be regarded as extravagance, the persons she draws entertain
> her whilst sitting, become her friends and continue to be so …

Unlike many an aspiring female artist at that time, Rolinda had the strength of purpose to subvert the prevailing view of art produced by women as being amateur and unworthy of attention; following her mother's example, she had a script to follow. Ellen valued the economic benefits of her daughter's chosen profession as much as the social. The diaries of the Royal Academician Joseph Farington provide evidence of a small number of women attempting to make a living on the edges of the art world between 1793 and 1821,[7] unfortunately without the great advantage of a role model like Ellen.

According to Ellen's journal, between February and April 1814 Rolinda worked on a self-portrait, which could be the image in Plate 4.1, showing a confident young woman in gauzy evening wear, with the bloom of youth and a wreath of flowers in her dark hair. As in the portrait of her mother at tea (Plate 4.2), this is more than a record of the artist's features: she presents herself as if turning from her piano, demonstrating her skills as a musician as well as a painter. She shades her eyes as she looks at us and adjusts her shawl with her right hand, giving the pose an air of immediacy.

A number of events around this time may have influenced the direction of some of Rolinda's work. In London the previous year she and Ellen had viewed, with the Cumberland family, Edward Bird's painting *The Surrender of Calais* (location unknown, print made by John Young after Edward Bird: British Museum, 1817). Bird had been honoured in 1813 by being appointed Historical Painter to Princess Charlotte. His painting *The Reading of the Will Concluded* (Bristol Museums, 1811) had caused such a stir at the Royal Academy when it was shown in 1811 that it had to be roped off.[8]

On their 1813 London trip Ellen and Rolinda had also visited the studios of the American artists John Singleton Copley and Benjamin West, their American experience providing a common bond. These painters produced works that treated historical and contemporary subjects realistically. At the time of Ellen and Rolinda's visit West was also President of the Royal Academy (despite incurring suspicion as a possible Democrat).

These specific works and artists showed what could be achieved with compositions that involved many people whose portraits had all been sketched from life, and mother and daughter were greatly impressed. The enthusiastic public reception of such paintings may have inspired Rolinda to embark on this more complex form of art – paintings of everyday life known as genre paintings, and the recording of contemporary events – as we shall see later in this chapter. Maria Spilsbury (1777–1820) was the only other female artist painting contemporary group scenes in Britain in the first decades of the nineteenth century. Instructed in her father's engraving studio, many of her paintings have an evangelical theme reflecting her family's Moravian faith. She had exhibited at the Royal Academy before moving to Ireland in 1813.[9]

From 1815 Rolinda's voice is heard in Ellen's journal for the first time. Much of the journal from this date is composed of material from Rolinda's journals and notebooks which her mother copied at a later date, with occasional notes and reflections from Ellen. At the end of 1815, Ellen wrote:

> *Copied from my dear Rolinda's Diaries or rather occasional Memorandums written in books of various sizes, her numerous pursuits and very active life being opposed to a regular noting down of the occurrences of each day as she had intended.*

As Ellen's comment above suggests, Rolinda's writing was never as discursive as her mother's and is mainly in note form, but she started out with good intentions:

> *The advantages of a faithful journal are many: recording all the right and wrong actions of the day would tend to prevent the wrong actions from being so frequently committed: would not the dislike of reading I have done nothing today of which my conscience can approve have some influence in preventing the repetition of such a day? And might not the pleasure derived from the reflection of spending a day well lead to doing so again?*

It was around this time that Rolinda wrote of beginning a portrait 'of myself at the easel' with 'mamma looking on' – her *The Artist and Her Mother* of 1816 (Plate 4.3). This double portrait shows the artist at work with the tools of her trade: palette,brush and maulstick in one hand, her painting hand resting on the maulstick, framed by the frilled cuff of her sleeve. The subject of her painting appears to be a young woman with a small horse, perhaps drawn from one of the sketches she had recently been making of her friends in the characters of country girls. The mother-and-daughter portrait is a confident statement: Rolinda holds the viewer's gaze with composure, while the framed canvases behind her indicate her status and productivity. Her mother admires the painting from behind the easel, her head placed intimately near to her daughter's. As well as a portrayal of Rolinda as a working artist, this is also a tribute to Ellen's unfailing support and guidance.

The use of a self-portrait to declare one's professional status was something several European women artists had done, but in Britain there are few such examples. Mary Beale (bap. 1633, d. 1699), in her self-portrait of *c.*1666, and Angelica Kauffmann (1741–1807) in hers of *c.*1770–75 (both in the National Portrait Gallery) are two. Ellen observed: 'My dear Rolinda was pursuing her profession with the greatest ardour, most desirous to attain excellence.'

## ELLEN'S OWN WORK DEVELOPS

With Rolinda's practice becoming firmly established, Ellen – now heading for her later forties – was feeling able to leave her daughter's side. In 1816 Ellen received a commission from some old friends. It is likely that, visiting the Darwins at their family home, The Mount, in Shrewsbury, she made portraits there of Dr Robert Darwin and a double-portrait of his son, the young Charles Darwin, along with his sister Emily Catherine – this was the first portrait ever painted of Charles (Plate 4.4). This latter may have been to celebrate Charles's upcoming seventh birthday on 12 February 1816. The plant he is holding has been identified as probably being *Lachenalia aloides*, the opal flower, a plant native to South Africa which would have been grown in The Mount's hothouse and had just come into flower.[10] She also made a portrait of his brother Erasmus aged 12, grandson of the same Erasmus whose painting had helped build the Sharples reputation in the US, and his sister Caroline, aged 16. These four portraits, painted the year before the death of Charles's mother Susannah, are the only works by Ellen Sharples on public display at the time of writing; they hang in the drawing room at Down House in Kent, the later home of Charles Darwin.

Plate 4.3

**ROLINDA SHARPLES**

*The Artist and Her Mother*

1816 | Oil on panel | 37 x 29 cm

Bristol Museums, Courtesy Bristol Culture

Plate 4.4

**ELLEN SHARPLES**

*Charles Darwin and His Sister Emily Catherine*

c.1816 | Pastel on paper | 37.5 x 34 cm (incl. frame)

Down House, Downe, Kent

Historic England Archive, Courtesy Darwin Heirlooms Trust

Two more of Ellen's portraits of children, with some similarities to the Darwin double portrait but undated, were sold in 2005. *Boy and Girl Standing in a Landscape*[11] presents two siblings in a pastoral scene: the boy, holding a cream top hat, is very formally dressed in a dark blue suit; his sister, in a white dress and yellow shoes, holds a basket of flowers. In *Two Children Wearing Pale Yellow Dresses*[12] the pose is by a window; the older child holds a hoop and stick, while the younger has a whip and a top. Another, single, portrait, *Portrait of a Young Boy*,[13] was sold in 2004 and shows a youth with a challenging gaze.

The recent appearance of a number of fine original portraits at various auction houses (a succession of them are detailed below) makes it clear that Ellen's work flourished in later life. Most are not dated but dates can be assumed by the age of the sitter – Ellen and Rolinda were evidently both working as artists simultaneously, Ellen into her late fifties. From 1815, the journal is entirely concerned with Rolinda's career, with Ellen either too self-effacing or too busy to document the many patrons that she herself was attracting.

Ellen developed a personal style quite different from her miniature portraits. Working at a scale of around 26 x 23 cm, her later portraits show more of the figure, often seated and presented in three-quarter or full-face view, with details of dress finely interpreted. She uses a restrained colour palette with a subtly graduated grey background, greatly enhancing the dramatic quality of the picture. A portrait of Lady William Cavendish Bentinck (1783–1843)[14] uses this technique, setting off the red of her fur-trimmed cloak; she wears a simple white dress and holds a book in her gloved hand. In the same art sale as the Bentinck was a portrait of an unnamed young lady in a white Regency dress, her black curls piled high in a jewelled comb, an orange shawl on one shoulder, and the curve of her neck highlighted by the dark background.[15] In *Portrait of a Lady* an older woman sits by a sewing table holding a piece of lace; she wears a high-necked lacy gown and an elaborate turban with roses tucked into it.[16]

In about 1820 Ellen made a striking portrait of the young Rt Hon. Russell Gurney QC (1804–1878), and another of Robert Faraday (1788–1846), brother of Michael Faraday.[17] In 1825 she captured the dashing Captain William Thomas Eardley Twistleton Fiennes standing in military dress.[18] Four more portraits, *The Reverend Charles Curtis*, *Timothy Curtis*, *Portrait of a Gentleman* and *John Claremont Whiteman*, a Commander in the East India Company, were sold at Sothebys between 2001 and 2003.[19] Two half-length oval portraits of Mr and Mrs Woodland[20] are in her earlier style.

Two portraits present subjects dear to Ellen's heart: reading and writing. A charming 1823 oil portrait shows the half-length figure of Henrietta Browne Clayton reading to her eight-year-old daughter Eleanor.[21] Originally from Lancashire,

Henrietta became a near neighbour of Ellen's in Clifton (Henrietta lived at Prince's Buildings); although this painting is attributed to Ellen it is more likely to be Rolinda's work, as there is no record of Ellen using oils. Rolinda would have been a similar age to Henrietta, and the relaxed intimacy of the pose implies that they could have been friends; the painting on an easel in the background suggests that she too was an artist. Ellen's *Young Lady Writing a Letter*[22] shows a young woman in white in mid-correspondence, her pen poised and a folded letter with red sealing wax on the table before her.

## ROLINDA'S FIRST PAINTING OF CONTEMPORARY LIFE

Meanwhile, Rolinda was preparing her most ambitious work so far:

> *In the course of the year 1817 she began the cloakroom at the ball, a group of 31 figure portraits finished in the year 1818. It attracted extraordinary attention during its progress. Mr Roberts, then Master of Ceremonies having an objection to sit she introduced Mr Pennington the preceding M.C.*

This is the first of Rolinda's multifigure compositions, and it shows a social event at Clifton's Assembly Rooms (Plate 4.5). In 1811, the Clifton Hotel and Assembly Rooms had opened just around the corner from the Sharples family home on Sion Hill. It was designed by Francis Greenway, who in 1812 had been convicted of forgery and transported to Australia, where he is now regarded as the father of Australian architecture, having designed over forty buildings in Sydney. The painting conveys the glamour and excitement of this important social occasion, with all the figures drawn from life. A Clifton Fancy Ball attended by Rolinda some years later was reported in the newspaper as follows, giving a flavour of the kind of event shown in her painting:

> *Company arrived at 9 o'clock, rooms fancifully decorated with flowers and shrubs, and an excellent band gave tone and life to the various waltzes, quadrilles and gallopades. It is vain attempting adequately to describe the brilliant effect produced by an assembly of 300 figures, richly and fancifully attired in costumes of various ages, traversing a splendidly illuminated room with all the grace and elegance of polished manners and then gaily moving in the spirited dance. One o'clock supper rooms thrown open, partook of luxurious banquet, every delicacy of the season. After supper dancing resumed with increased zest, and kept up with gaiety until four o'clock.*[23]

Plate 4.5

**ROLINDA SHARPLES**

*The Cloakroom, Clifton Assembly Rooms*

c.1818 | Oil on canvas | 73 x 88 cm

Bristol Museums, Courtesy Bristol Culture

This painting has become emblematic of the world of Jane Austen, whose novel *Pride and Prejudice* had been published in 1813. It shows acute observation of the social scene, providing a meticulous record of the fashions of the Regency period: men not in uniform are dressed in black; most of the young women wear white, with the older women in darker colours. Smiles and gossip are exchanged, and there are flirtatious glances. As the guests prepare for dancing, a maid in the foreground helps with a lady's overshoes, worn to protect her satin slippers from the dirt of the streets. The scene would have been a familiar one to Rolinda and she was perfectly qualified to interpret it.

## ROLINDA'S WORKING PRACTICE IS ESTABLISHED

The next 18 years of Rolinda's too-short life were a model of hard work and single-minded dedication to her art. She continued to receive many portrait commissions, working on these in between her genre scenes and history paintings.

Her assiduous work schedule was interspersed with piano practice and visits to Clifton Church. Evenings were spent sewing caps and bonnets for Ellen, sometimes singing, reading and playing chess. Occasionally there was a social event, a music recital or a party where they danced quadrilles. Ever the student, she continued to struggle with vulgar fractions and attended chemistry lectures.

In the wake of the great interest shown in the Assembly Rooms picture, a Mrs B. had asked Rolinda to make a painting of *A Concert* in her drawing room. Although this painting took up much of Rolinda's time it was never finished, as the controlling Mrs B. wished to choose so many of her friends to be in it. Whilst waiting for different people to pose, Rolinda started on a design for a picture of a market:

> *Rolinda became much interested in the picture: at six o'clock in the summer mornings she was at her easel, one morning at four I accompanied her to the market at Bristol where she made a sketch before the people were assembled.*

Mother and daughter were offered the use of a drawing room overlooking the market, where Rolinda could come and sketch the people at any time, while Ellen read at her side. *A Market* (present location unknown) was the first of Rolinda's pictures to receive national attention.

# NATIONAL RECOGNITION

Rolinda finished *A Market* early in 1820 and had it framed, together with four small pictures, ready for submission to the Royal Academy at Somerset House:

> *no time was to be lost, it was packed up and sent; myself, son and daughter soon followed, and arrived just in time to have it seen by a few Royal Academicians to whom we had letters, and to heighten a little the colour by glazing tints suggested by Mr Reinagle.*

But would the picture be selected?

> *Anxiety then arose whether it would be received, as we heard that hundreds of pictures were rejected every year … soon the agreeable intelligence came that all her pictures had been received, the next anxiety was where they would be hung, how would they look among the select performances of the most distinguished artists in the Kingdom?*

Their fears proved unfounded: 'First Monday in May [1820] the Exhibition opened to the publick. How great was our joy seeing Rolinda's [*Market*] picture placed most advantageously and … looking particularly attractive.' *A Market* was noticed in a review of the best pictures in the *Morning Advertiser* as 'full of incident, amongst the works in the higher department of the art'. Ellen and Rolinda found this 'very exhilarating', as were other reviews where *Eliza at Work*, another of the five pictures submitted, was noticed as 'professing considerable merit' (*Eliza at Work*: oil painting, location unknown; possible preparatory drawing/watercolour of a young woman peeling potatoes, Bristol Museums; the sitter may be Eliza Cumberland). The other three works exhibited were two studies of *Shells* and a *Portrait of a Lady*.

Ellen and Rolinda must have felt that at the age of 26 Rolinda was finally getting the respect she deserved. Visiting London to admire her exhibits, they made frequent trips to Somerset House to see the crowds around *A Market*: 'similar to crowds around "The Reading of a Will" by Wilkie, the "Wolf and Lamb" by Mulready, "Londoners Gypsying" by Leslie and a few other paintings by distinguished artists'.

# MOVING HOUSE

On their return to Clifton from the capital, building work was being carried out on the house, so – feeling rather flat after London – Ellen, James Jnr and Rolinda made an excursion to the Wye Valley and Tintern, where all three of them sketched the Romantic landscapes. That autumn a new possibility arose:

> we saw two new houses nearby in Clifton at Lower Harley Place, built by
> Mr Warne ... one, just the wished for size, commanding extensive rural views
> north, east and west, pleased us all so much as to decide me to engage it for five
> or seven years with the privilege of purchasing it at a certain price. Mr W. was
> very accommodating and allowed folding doors to be made between the two
> drawing rooms, and the garden in front to be laid out according to our taste.
> It was expeditiously furnished and Rolinda in a room selected for her painting
> room was soon ardently engaged: her brother, in another room of his choice
> equally interested in resuming his profession of portrait painting.

At the new house (Fig. 5), on Clifton Down opposite the Mall, Rolinda's steady flow of portrait commissions continued, while she also worked up her small genre scenes and developed ideas for larger canvases. Her paintings began to be regularly accepted at the Royal Academy.[24] In 1822 *Rownham Ferry, with Portraits*[25] was exhibited, along with a painting entitled *The Young Delinquent* (location of both unknown).

*Rownham Ferry* is one of her most charming pictures, a lively and cheerful scene full of expression and social detail, showing people in holiday mood waiting with musical instruments and baskets of food to take the short boat trip across the Avon, to picnic in Nightingale Valley or to walk to Ashton and eat strawberries. It shows the Avon Gorge before Brunel's Suspension Bridge was built, as well as St Vincent's Rock and the St Vincent's Parade of terraced houses, where the family was later to live and where Ellen was to end her days.

The family must have been greatly upset by a scathing account of the exhibition which appeared in *John Bull*, a Sunday newspaper famous for its 'witty criticism'. Rolinda's painting was a particular target:

> 'Rownham Ferry' by Rolinda Sharples, a view illustrated by caricatures of the
> inhabitants of the neighbourhood, out of drawing and finished in a style that
> ought to have cost a little girl of eight years old a whipping. We really cannot
> understand why such abominable trash is admitted.[26]

Despite the crushing review the painting was sold three years later.

In 1823 the Bristol Institution for the Advancement of Science, Literature and the Arts opened in grand premises at the bottom of Bristol's Park Street (now a Freemasons' Masonic Lodge). Rolinda may have seen there the work of the Dutch genre painter Adriaen van Ostade (1610–1685), and paintings of his such as *The Cottage Dooryard* (National Gallery of Art, Washington, 1673) could have influenced her *The Village Gossips* (Bristol Museums, *c.*1828). The Bristol iron founder and art patron Daniel Wade Acraman, whose warehouse is now the home of the city's Arnolfini art centre, was also making a collection of Flemish and Dutch paintings by Teniers, Weenix and Van Ostade, which she may have been aware of.

Rolinda worked at several paintings at one time, moving between them as circumstances dictated. She often continued to retouch paintings for extended periods, even after they had been exhibited, perhaps indicating some lack of confidence; this makes stating their exact dates difficult. Her brief notes indicate the seriousness of her practice and her determination to achieve the effects she wanted, with technical experiments if needed. In spring 1823, while working on *A Mouse!* (location unknown, 1825) and *Blowing the Candle* (Plate 4.6), she started making 'contrivances' in preparation for her painting *St James's Fair* (also called *Bristol Fair*, original: Private Collection; copy: M Shed, Bristol Museums; both *c.*1825).

Fig. 5
*No. 2 Lower Harley Place*
Clifton | Sharples home 1820–31

Plate 4.6

ROLINDA SHARPLES

*Blowing the Candle*

c.1822–3 | Oil on canvas | 70 x 90 cm

Bristol Museums, Courtesy Bristol Culture

With her father's practical approach she made a model in pasteboard of a cara-van, and worked on perspective drawings. She contrived a lay figure, the kind of jointed model of a human figure that artists use, which she was thinking of having someone construct for her. After puzzling for some time over how to create the shoulder joint, she worked it out, sending for a carpenter who undertook to make it. She noted her preoccupations:

> Nov. 14TH ... *commenced* A Mouse – *alarm created by the intrusion of the little animal into a drawing room, regretted the panel was not of a larger size.*
>
> DECEMBER 4TH *In the morning at the Mouse Group, in the evening at the Candlelight piece ⌈Blowing the Candle⌉, doing very little good as I could not please myself in regard to the dress of Celia.* 9TH *Contrived the dress for Celia in the candle piece; then laid a second coat of paint on the green cloth in the Mouse Group. Evening applied to the Candle group.*

JAN. 4TH *Painted the red silk drapery, and was just finishing the white when I conclude to rub it out, and dispose the folds differently [for* Blowing the Candle*]. Reading, chess and music.* 8TH ... *varnished* Rownham Ferry. 10TH ... *day cold and disagreeable, snowing.* 12TH ... *went to St Michaels. Mr Spencer delivered an excellent discourse.*

MARCH 1ST *Miss Cave sat for the hair in the picture of the fainting lady in the Mouse group. Walked to Bristol, Mrs Maze lent me charades and riddles.* 13TH *Walked down the new Zig Zag [a steep and winding footpath which had just opened down the side of the Avon Gorge]. Making models for Fair. Little Drew stood with a hearth brush in his hand, to destroy or drive away the mouse. Received a letter from Felix and wrote one to him and sent my picture and a box of silk papers by the brig Mary.*

This was the last time the family was to hear from Felix.

It may be around this time that Rolinda painted *A Domestic Interior with a Gentlemen's Shaving Ritual Interrupted by His Wife*, a rather mysterious semi-comic example of her genre scenes, for sale at the time of writing.[27] A label on the reverse reads 'Mrs Rolinda Sharples, 2 Lower Harley Place, Clifton'. It shows her experimenting with different emotions and facial expressions. In the picture, a woman in a large hat seizes her half-shaved husband as a barber sharpens his razor; a distressed older woman with a dog looks on. *A Dentist Pulling a Tooth*, by the Flemish painter David Teniers, is a possible influence; the painting was in the Acraman collection around that time.[28]

*A Mouse!* was exhibited at the Royal Academy in 1824, and reviews were good in several publications. Rolinda received an enthusiastic request from Carlisle to send it there for exhibition, together with *A Market*. The *Carlisle Patriot* published many compliments, and she became the toast of the town's newly founded Carlisle Academy of Arts. Work resumed on *St James's Fair*, which she finished in 1825. The historic fair had an unsavoury reputation, and the subject had been used as a vehicle for moral comment in a painting by Samuel Colman the year before. Rolinda's is a somewhat sanitised interpretation: ordinary families on a fun day out.

Also in 1825, she exhibited for the first time at the newly formed Society of British Artists at their gallery in London's Suffolk Street, Pall Mall, and was thrilled when a Dr Mackey, 'a gentleman of large fortune' from Cumberland, bought *St James's Fair* for 180 guineas. Wishing to see more of her work, he also bought *Rownham Ferry* and *A Market* for 100 guineas each and *A Mouse!* (being half the size) for 50 guineas. He announced his intention of forming a gallery of British painters near Keswick in Cumberland, and said that 'a series of Miss Sharples paintings, like those of Hogarth, would become one of the attractions of the lakes'.

Full of praise, Dr Mackey asked for her ideas for a new painting. Immensely flattered, Rolinda suggested '"suspension of payment at a Bank" as well suited to a great variety of expression; which he approvingly immediately gave her a commission'. This turned out to be an ironic choice of subject, for after working on it exclusively for two years and turning down all portrait commissions, no more was heard from Dr Mackey. On exhibition in London in 1827 (though Rolinda continued work on it until 1831), *The Stoppage of the Bank* (Plate 4.7) attracted great interest and favourable reviews, but the charming Dr Mackey had lost all his money in Mexican bonds. Rolinda resumed her portraits once more with the many clients who had waited so patiently for her.

The buildings in *Stoppage* are based on ones from central Bristol: the seventeenth-century Dutch House and buildings in Corn Street including the Church of All Saints. The bank of Browne, Cavanagh, Browne & Bayly, known as the Bristol Bullion Bank, of 37 Corn Street, stopped payments in 1822.[29] The painting's composition shows the influence of E.V. Rippingille, whose work *A Country Post Office* Rolinda would have seen at the Royal Academy in 1819 (later copy by Rippingille: Lotherton Hall, Leeds Museums and Galleries, 1829). This was the beginning of a period of bank collapses, and despite her comfortable life now, Ellen had been permanently scarred by imprisonment in France and was never to feel financially secure, so it was a subject with particular resonance for Rolinda. It was a significant departure for her to paint a scene which addressed the impact of a major economic event on the women and children in the sorrowing family groups she portrayed, and it extended the range of subject matter which female artists were prepared to address.

In December 1827 Rolinda was unanimously elected as an Honorary Member of the Society of British Artists, the highest honour to be bestowed on a female artist in the UK up to this point – the term 'honorary' indicating that they viewed her status as being non-professional. There were notable showings of her work in the mid-1820s and beyond. *The Stoppage of the Bank* was exhibited in Liverpool, Leeds and Birmingham, and she exhibited works in Carlisle (1824–6 and 1830) and Southampton (1828–9). *Blowing the Candle* and *The Village Gossips* were exhibited in Dublin and Leeds in 1829. The former is a good example of how far she had come – this dramatic painting with its subtle light effects is one of Rolinda's most delightful genre scenes, all the more effective for its close-up framing and concentration on character (Plate 4.6). At long last her work began to be recognised in her home town: *Stoppage* was exhibited at the Bristol Institution 'with an abundance of compliments and praise'. Ellen took great pride in her daughter's achievements, and hoped for a brilliant future.

Plate 4.7

**ROLINDA SHARPLES**

*The Stoppage of the Bank*

c.1825–31 | Oil on panel | 84 x 120.5 cm

Bristol Museums, Courtesy Bristol Culture

Plate 5.1

**ROLINDA SHARPLES**

*Mrs Ellen Sharples*

1836? | Oil on canvas | 91 x 72.5 cm

RWA (Royal West of England Academy), Bristol

CHAPTER FIVE

# Rolinda and Ellen's Later Years, Late 1820s–49

ROLINDA'S ELEVATION TO membership of the Society of British Artists could not have come at a better time, raising her spirits after the disappointment over the elusive Dr Mackey. Always seeking self-improvement, in November 1827 she and Ellen plucked up courage for a new experience:

> *after some consultation on the subject Mamma and I went to Mr Esthin's lectures on anatomy, determining if there were very few ladies not to go into the room; it was however crowded with ladies. Many well prepared specimens were exhibited which were handled without apparent reluctance by the fair sex. Ladies had been particularly requested to attend.*

It is worth noting that this was some thirty years before women were, for example, able to attend anatomy classes at the Philadelphia Fine Arts Academy (in 1860).[1]

In the autumn of 1828 Rolinda ventured into Somerset to make a landscape painting: *Cheddar* (Bristol Museums). The Sharples journal records:

> SEPT. 9TH *Set off for Cheddar with Miss Shipperdson. Rocks very beautiful.*

> SEPT. 10T*h Began a view: rained more or less every day during the week we remained, had to sit in the wet painting during the intervals between the showers.*

> SEPT. 29TH *Began an enlarged copy of Cheddar on panel.*

In 1829 she began preparations for her picture, *The Clifton Race-course* of 1830–36 (M Shed, Bristol Museums). Held every year at Durdham Down – part of Bristol's long-established area of open land called The Downs – the horse races, like the balls at the Assembly Rooms, were considered important social events where many of her friends and prospective patrons were seen. Rolinda's research was as meticulous as always, with days spent at Ashton Court estate sketching the carriage and four horses of its owner, Sir John Smyth, proving especially delightful, including a lunch provided with all sorts of delicacies: 'partridges and pineapples, hot house grapes and other luxuries'. Ashton Court was located in Long Ashton just over the river from Clifton and Smyth was one of her patrons (see Rolinda Sharples, *Sir John Smyth*, Bristol Museums, 1829). Smyth's ancestors had owned Jamaican sugar plantations, and this grand house, like so many in Bristol, was built on the profits of the slave trade. She still found time for her studies in science, however: 'attended Mr Adam's course of lectures on chemistry, illustrated by very beautiful experiments'.

At the turn of the decade, in the family tradition, Rolinda took stock of her achievements, listing the large number of portraits she had completed:

> *arranged my colours, reckoned up my accounts, cold very severe.*
> *The prospect before the house presents a dreary extent of snow varied only*
> *by the dark leafless hedges and trees, and the distant houses at Redland,*
> *which however are frequently obscured by fog; now and then a sportsman*
> *making many ineffectual pops.*

On 1 January 1830: 'The Rev. Sidney [sic] Smith called on us. He and his family have taken possession of the house in Gloucester Row [in Clifton].' On 21 January: 'Retouched the picture Mr S. Smith sat for yesterday' (*Reverend Sydney Smith*, Bristol Museums). Smith, celebrated wit and champion of parliamentary reform, was a canon at Bristol Cathedral; his daughter Saba and Rolinda were friends. Other activities noted in the journal around this time included retouching *The Stoppage of the Bank* and Rolinda spending evenings sewing a cap for her mother while Ellen read from a novel by Walter Scott. They also held a musical party at which Rolinda played Haydn, while in addition she was

> *engaged almost every day at the races [i.e. working on The Clifton*
> *Race-course, including out and about doing studies from life] ... in our*
> *walk overtaken by a violent snowstorm, sheltered until out of patience,*
> *borrowed umbrellas, wind too high to keep them up, never out on so*
> *disagreeable day ... contrived two figures at the races, but I get on very*
> *slowly in my painting this cold weather.*

'The races', *The Clifton Race-course*, continued to occupy her through the spring ('still at the perspective lines in the race picture'), working from early morning at figure studies in her studio or out on the Downs; even sketching in the rain. In July of 1830 she made a rare contact with one of Bristol's artistic community: 'called to see young Muller's picture, a very promising picture for so young an artist'. Eighteen-year-old William Müller, whose father was the curator of the Bristol Institution, painted Romantic landscapes based on drawings made during gentlemen's evening sketching parties.

Rolinda had already broken new ground for female artists by tackling the subject of the social consequences of a bank failure in *Stoppage*. Ideas for more themes from outside her own sheltered existence began to occur, as she noted the increasingly turbulent political tensions in Bristol.

Looking at the journal, she seems both intrigued and appalled by such events. On 24 July: Acland was haranguing the populace on the top of Brandon Hill. On our return met the mob: Acland in an open carriage, flags flying, music playing. Mr Fairbrother accompanied us home.' James Acland was the publisher of The Bristolian, a newspaper exposing the abuses of the Corporation of Bristol and the Courts and demanding reform of the national political system. Seen by the authorities as a troublemaker, he had been imprisoned the year before but was now standing for Parliament, fighting for one of the two seats which then represented the whole of Bristol – one traditionally Tory, the other Whig.

On 27 July:

> *Evening called on Mrs Adair at Bristol, sad rioting there. Mr Acland passed the window standing on a fly [a light carriage] looking very silly, preceded by flags and music, and followed by several of the lower and lowest people.*

On 30 July Rolinda went to see the hustings, and to sketch the crowd at a distance. On 2 August: 'went to Queen Square [central Bristol], and at Mr Maze's I again sketched distant figures. The crowd was immense, banners and flags waving, music etc'. On 4 and 5 August: 'again at Bristol sketching, walked round the hustings, and saw, and heard, Davis, Baily and Acland addressing the assembled multitude'.

Richard Hart Davis was the Tory sitting Member for this parliamentary election, while the traditionally Whig seat was contested by the anti-slavery candidate Edward Protheroe and James Evan Baillie. Rivalry between opposing bands of supporters was intense, with occasional outbursts of violence. On 4 May 1831 Rolinda

> *went to see the chairing of Mr Bailie [sic] and Mr Prothero [sic] from Mr Maze's window, who being true blue objected to other colours being displayed. The various flags and emblems had a pretty effect, the chairs were particularly splendid; regretted I had not colours with me. Began a sketch of the scene afterwards from remembrance.*

Rolinda does not disclose her own political sympathies – she writes elsewhere of not being a politician.

# A CHANGE OF ADDRESS

S ince the beginning of 1831 Ellen had been considering buying a house in Park Place, at the top of Bristol's Park Street and nearer to the city centre than their present home. However, considering the uncertainty of the stock market (the 'Navy 5 per cents' she had invested in after James's death had fallen in value), and ever cautious, she decided to leave the heights of Clifton, and their rented home at Lower Harley Place, and instead rent a house in Hotwells, 60 metres below and beside the river Avon:

Fig. 6
*No. 3 St Vincent's Parade*
Hotwells, Bristol | Sharples home | 1831–49

*Mama concluded to take a house in St Vincent's Parade. We are to have a key*
*to the shrubbery behind the house which leads up to Sion Hill in one direction,*
*and to Windsor Terrace in another, very pretty and commands beautiful*
*views … Met Mrs German who thinks our house will be too hot, afterwards*
*Mr Street who thinks it will be too cold.*

Number 3 St Vincent's Parade (Fig. 6), at the end of a terrace of nine houses and now known as 372 Hotwell Road, overlooked a treelined promenade leading to what had been, in the 1700s, the heart of a successful spa designed to rival that of Bath. Now fading in popularity, at its peak the spa had brought the fashionable flocking to its pump room at Hotwell House (demolished in 1822) to take the 'cure' of the hot spring waters for their ailments or for fashion's sake and to parade along the promenade. Hard to imagine now as traffic thunders along the Portway.

At the end of May 1831 Rolinda made the last finishing touches to *Stoppage*. Mr Warne, their landlord and friend at Lower Harley Place, allowed them to take any plants from the garden that they pleased. After many renovations that they were having done at St Vincent's Parade, moving day came on 14 June:

*James and I, and Fanny [possibly a friend or maid] came first, six men busily*
*engaged. Mr Osborn with a cart and horses, Mr Fox with a hand barrow.*
*Went up in the afternoon to Lower Harley Place, Mamma returned with me*
*in the evening, both excessively tired. All week engaged with unpacking.*

They delighted in the view of the woods and rocks opposite: 'we continue to be pleased with St Vincent's Parade: the sailing of all kinds of vessels, and the variety of figures passing the windows affords us much amusement'.

Ellen would later (1843) write to her friend Miss Harriet Pigott (the author Harriet Pigott, of *Records of Real Life in the Palace and the Cottage*, 1839):

*the pictures appeared to more advantage in rooms spacious and lofty, and the*
*rent was not quite so high. The ferry at Rownham so near we crossed almost*
*every summer afternoon with light camp chairs, and a simple apparatus*
*of Rolinda's contrivance, to enable her in oil colours to sketch from nature.*
*In Leigh Woods, Salvator Rosa and Nightingale valleys how delighted we*
*were, breathing the delicious air, and observing the beautiful picturesque*
*scenery as it was marked permanently on the panel, to be conveyed to any other*
*place. Every sound and every object around spoke of peace and happiness: it*
*seemed that there could be nothing of evil or misery in the world.*

Leigh Woods opened into the Nightingale valley and Salvator Rosa valley, the latter woodland glen earning its name for being reminiscent of the Romantic landscapes of the Italian artist. Rolinda, too, is here seen recording her surroundings solely in terms of their visual effect – an effect very much imbued with the dominant philosophy of landscape art at that time as reflecting contemporary concepts of the Romantic, picturesque, beautiful and sublime:

> *one day going to Bristol saw a rowing match, a very amusing scene, figures*
> *on the rigging of ships etc. One day walked to see the coal works near Ashton,*
> *a very picturesque building with very picturesque machinery.*

But political events were soon to shatter her Romantic view of the world. In the autumn of 1831 the Bristol Riots erupted. These events were to inspire one of Rolinda's most important paintings, and the sensation they caused in the Sharples household is clear from her account, which runs to several pages in her notebook (then copied into Ellen's journal).

## RIOTS IN BRISTOL

T he great political question of the time was Reform, a campaign to extend the number of people entitled to vote, then only five per cent of the population. This divided opinion like nothing else. Lack of trade in the port of Bristol, food shortages, the bank failures, cholera, the weather – all were attributed to the failure to pass or not to pass the Bill.

The second Reform Bill had just been voted down in the House of Lords, stalling the Bill's progress through the House. Reaction to this was beginning to erupt in the cities not well represented in Parliament. Journalled on 29 October 1831:

> *A great mob in Bristol owing to Sir Charles Wetheral [sic] coming into the*
> *city, he was obliged to take refuge in the bottom of the carriage. It is said that a*
> *man has been killed.*

Wetherell was a senior Bristol judge and MP for Boroughbridge in Yorkshire, representing just 48 men. He had stated in Parliament that the people of Bristol were opposed to the Bill, when in fact a petition of 17,000 signatures had been collected to support it. Later that night Wetherell escaped in disguise from Bristol's Mansion House (home of the Lord Mayor in Queen Square) across the roofs and fled to London. On 30 October Rolinda noted: 'On James's return from Bristol, where he had been to church, this morning he saw a large mob collected near Reeve's Hotel, yelling, throwing stones etc., and he heard distant shots from the military.'

This same day, the 30th, the family continued with their plans to dine with their friends the Lidiards in Bristol but

> on entering the front drawing room we saw flames at a distance, which we were informed proceeded from the New Gaol. After dinner these flames subsided and new ones broke out. Reports came that Lawford's Gate, Bridewell and the Mansion House were burning.

Feeling very anxious, they sent for a fly to take them home whilst they still could, with their host accompanying them.

> There was something awful in the flames, and the perfect stillness, not a bell was rung in any of the churches, as is usual in accidental fires … just as we had got home Mrs Maze came in the greatest agitation telling us that the mansion house and the whole south side of the square [Queen Square] was in flames, an immense mob collected, and they expected their house would be down before morning. They had secured nothing of material value. In her haste she had only taken her watch, and a few trinkets, the horses and carriage could not be got out of the stable. After changing her shoes and stockings which were wet through and taking a glass of wine, she became more tranquil. We proposed that she should stay with us during the night, she however preferred going over on the ferry to Rownham Lodge.

Mr Maze Junior soon arrived with the news that the Mayor, Charles Pinney, a Whig and a supporter of the Bill, would not give permission for the soldiers to fire on the incendiaries, and that the Bishop's Palace and the Cathedral were threatened.

Journal entry for 31 October:

> After an almost sleepless night of alarm, sometimes watching the inflamed sky from the back of the house, sometimes fancying the voices of the mob approaching, and with a thousand imaginary fears, morning at length dawned … small groups of anxious enquirers were at almost every door, strangers accosted one another without the ceremony of introduction, terror and dismay were depicted on every countenance.

They heard that their friends the Mazes' house was safe, but that their ex-neighbour Mr Franklyn had two teeth knocked out attempting to save the Bishop's Palace. The rioters had broken open Acraman's Iron Works, taken sledgehammers and then forced open the doors of the gaol to set the prisoners free; apparently this was witnessed by a troop of soldiers who gave three cheers and rode away.

The prisoners then

> proceeded to the square [Queen Square], [and] plundered and set fire to
> the houses with shouts of fiendish joy on each new exploit, until two sides of
> the square were completely destroyed, many however perished in their own
> created fires.

Rolinda and Ellen were horrified at this breakdown of law and order and the reports
of the behaviour of their fellow citizens:

> whilst the fires were extending the horrid monsters, men and women, were
> regaling with [sic] the stolen wines, and spirits, the details of eye witnesses are
> too revolting, and it is with pain that facts so near home convince us that so
> much depravity can exist.

Feeling fearful and unsettled, they called on their friends and neighbours, hearing
that all the gentlemen of Clifton had been sworn in as constables. Fighting had
been going on for some time in Bristol, and the soldiers were only just getting the
mob under control; the slaughter was dreadful. Coming home from these calls they
heard alarming reports that the cavalry had been riding over heaps of the slain:

> At night constables, gentlemen, tradesmen etc. with guns, pistols, swords rusty
> and bright, commenced their duty of guarding persons and property. There is
> a large party of them on our parade. One of the gentlemen constables knocked
> at our door, and requested us in case the gas lights should be put out to place
> candles in the windows, as otherwise should there be an affray they might shoot
> one another.

Another anxious night followed on 31 October:

> the sky indicated that fires still raged … guns popped off, windows rattled in
> the wind, a steam packet stuck in the mud, and the noise of the paddles sounded
> like distant drums: we were if possible more frightened than the night before.

The morning of 1 November brought accounts of sixty or seventy men killed and
many wounded taken to hospital. Various tales from the affrays abounded:

> one side of the square [Queen Square] is said to have been saved by a black
> man who shot one villain dead that was entering the house, another he
> succeeded in forcing out, and a woman who got in to plunder, he threw out of
> a window.

On 4 November Ellen and Rolinda ventured into Bristol to witness the destruction:

> *the scene in Queen Square is appalling, quite different from accidental fires,*
> *which are generally extinguished before the walls are so entirely injured, but*
> *here the fronts of the houses with the exception of one or two that are bent*
> *inwards, and are in a tottering condition, have fallen in and are a mass*
> *of bricks; the walls that remain are broken in a variety of fantastic shapes,*
> *the pillars of the Custom House stand upright and alone …*

Rolinda was too disturbed by the scene to draw: 'we saw two artists sketching this ruin, but such subjects for the pencil are not sufficiently agreeable, and too much connected with horrible impressions'.

## THE TRIAL OF THOMAS BRERETON

After a brief respite working quietly at *The Clifton Race-course* picture, in January 1832 two friends arrived with tickets for the court martial of Lieutenant-Colonel Thomas Brereton, urging Rolinda to make a sketch of the scene. Brereton, of the 14th Dragoons, faced 11 charges. Some thought he could have done more to prevent the destruction of the city; others that he had tried to restrain his soldiers from violence against the rioters and was being made a scapegoat for the failure of the city magistrates.

Rolinda went along and sketched many of the principal players in the drama. For example:

> *Capt. Warrington, an interesting looking young man, appeared quite cheerful*
> *at his trial, took notes of the evidence, [and] cross questioned the witnesses,*
> *with as much unconcern as if he was counsel for the prisoner instead of being*
> *prisoner himself.*

(Warrington was later cashiered – dismissed without honour.)

She expressed her sympathy for

> *the poor and much pitied Col. Brereton: he sat with his arms folded with a*
> *countenance of hopeless abstraction. He rose, gave an almost inaudible answer*
> *of approval to whatever the President proposed, again folded his arms, and*
> *glanced his large full eye round the court. In my small book I had taken pencil*
> *sketches of poor Brereton, whose earthly tribunal was so dreadfully terminated.*

Ellen and Rolinda were not in court on the fifth day, 13 January, when General Dalbiac announced that the unfortunate Lieutenant-Colonel had shot himself, leaving his wife and four children. Facing the almost certain verdict against him, he had taken the option traditionally open to officers and gentlemen. Many of the officers shed tears.

Interest in the trial was intense, and despite the crowds Rolinda returned the next morning with her mother and stood at a window for six hours, although 'Mama was so pressed upon and annoyed by the crowd that she made her escape and returned home.' The trial became the sensation of the city, and despite arriving very early the next day mother and daughter had to wait in the crowd:

> *but we were amused by the conversation of two gentlemen, just before us,*
> *who were detailing the tricks by which some persons had effected an entrance*
> *without tickets, many of which were said to be forged ... the gentlemen called*
> *and knocked, and knocked and called, at length to my astonishment a loud*
> *voice behind the door called out is Miss and Mrs Sharples there? And to my*
> *surprise the impatient gentleman answered yes. Then, Capt. Protheroe, if you*
> *will take care of Mrs and Miss Sharples you shall be admitted ... with this*
> *introduction from my friend behind the door, Capt. P. offered me his arm ...*
> *to our friends Gen. and Mrs Brown we owed this privilege of admission.*

They were given their choice of places.

Rolinda received offers of sittings with all the main characters and made a coloured sketch of the proceedings: 'My sketches are creating quite a sensation, note after note being written to request permission to see them: my friends much wish me to paint or lithographise a Ct. M. [Court Martial].' She may have also been inspired in this work by George Hayter's painting *The Trial of Queen Caroline 1820* (National Portrait Gallery, 1820–23).

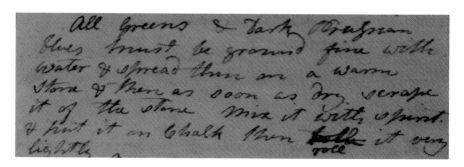

**EXCERPT FROM ELLEN SHARPLES'S NOTEBOOK**  All greens and dark Prussian blues must be ground fine with water and spread them on a warm stone and then as soon as dry scrape it of [sic] the stone. Mix it with spirit and put it on chalk then roll it very lightly

# A SPECIAL VISITOR

In March 1832 Rolinda's attention was diverted away from her work by the arrival from Philadelphia of a Mr Gerard Ralston, an acquaintance from their last American visit, who was on a tour of Europe. Rolinda was very taken with this intelligent and agreeable young man, who received more attention in her journal entries than any other gentleman of her acquaintance. He dined with them several times, and:

> he accompanied us to the Master of Ceremonies ball, where I danced with him, as also at Mrs Kelson's party on the 15th ... Mr Ralston has written a paper respecting the State of Pennsylvania where numerous workmen are wanted in the formation of railways for which Messrs Ralston's who are merchants, are to furnish all the iron ... Mr Ralston is intimately acquainted with Miss Edgeworth ... One day walked with Mama, James and Mr Ralston in Leigh Woods, through Salvator Rosa's valley, Nightingale valley and on our return round Clifton. Mr R. read us a letter from Miss Edgeworth, and took leave of us on the 31st.

Ellen and Rolinda were readers and admirers of Maria Edgeworth (1768–1849), a novelist and educationalist. Two of her sisters had married the subjects of portraits by the Sharples family: Emmeline had married their friend Dr John King (King's portrait was done by James Jnr and his children had probably been among Rolinda's first portraits), and Anna had married Dr Thomas Beddoes, a subject of James Snr's who had entertained the literati with nitrous oxide experiments at his Pneumatic Institution in Dowry Square. Maria had lived in Clifton herself in the 1790s, when she had complained of being unable to get a reader's ticket at the Bristol Library used by Coleridge, Southey and W.S. Landor, 'for no ladies go to the library'.[2]

After Mr R.'s departure Rolinda watched from her window as many ships full of emigrants headed for the Atlantic, on another day noting that she had encountered three wagonloads of people from Frome emigrating to America. Her observations around this period are the only hint in her journal entries of a possible romantic interest in her diligent and studious life. Later in the year Mr Ralston's sister-in-law, who was of delicate health, and her mother Mrs Wiggin visited Clifton, where 'they became very intimate'; Rolinda even introduced their portraits into her court martial painting. But of the dashing Gerard Ralston no more was heard. In 1838 he married the young Isabel Crawshay, daughter of William Crawshay of the Cyfarthfa Ironworks in Merthyr Tydfil, which exported much of the iron for the burgeoning American railway network in which the Ralstons were involved.

Returning to her easel at the end of March, Rolinda began work on *The Trial of Colonel Brereton* (completed 1834, M Shed, Bristol Museums). This was to be her most complex and ambitious painting, at a couple of metres' length, and her main focus for the next two years, between the portrait commissions which were her regular source of income. She spent several mornings drawing the interior of the Merchants' Hall (then in King Street, central Bristol), where she set her painting, although the trial did not take place there.[3] As she sketched the chandeliers, preparations for a great dinner were taking place: 'Mr T. showed us the kitchens where at two immense fires several saddles of mutton were roasting. Ready for the spit were many turkeys … piles of fowls for boiling, tongues etc.'

In May of 1832 political unrest broke out once more, and Rolinda noticed 'groups of anxious countenances conversing on the Reform Bill, an amendment being supported by a majority of 35', the next day noting that 'Lord Grey [the Whig Prime Minister] is said to have resigned, heard that 20, some say 40,000 people collected on Brandon Hill to discuss the bill.' The following evening she called on her friend Miss Shipperdson,

> who was in dreadful alarm lest the failure of the Bill should cause a
> revolution. Political unions assembling all over England, and numerous
> meetings of various classes, who threaten not to pay taxes unless the bill passes.

After an evening excursion to a lecture by Dr Riley, illustrated by beautiful specimens of various species of lizard, on 16 May she heard a report that the Reform Bill had passed, 'the mail having come in decked with laurels'. This turned out not to be true, but Lord Grey was once again in office. One evening at the theatre she observed that, during the playing of 'God Save the King', 'there was much hissing, and three men in the pit sat with their hats on during the whole of the performance'. The Bill received royal assent on 7 June, and on 18 June Rolinda attended the Reform procession and made some very rough sketches, observing that 'the banners and implements of trade were very inferior to those displayed on the coronation day. The political union were a sad shabby set.'

In July she remarked on the gorgeous sunsets during long evening walks on the Downs, but later in the month there was 'nothing talked of at the Commercial Rooms but the cholera … there had been 26 cases in Bristol, 9 of which had proved fatal … to the library … any mention of the cholera makes Mr A. choleric'. (The Commercial Rooms was a social club for merchants in Bristol's Corn Street; what Rolinda heard is likely to be local gossip, as she would not have gone there.) A friend called by who had been stopped by a fish woman in the street, with

> *please ma'am may I be so bold as to ax [sic] you what your gown is made
> of? ... of watered silk ... It be beautiful, if I was a lady I would have just
> such a one.*

Rolinda's friend made some observation to the woman about her making a fortune by selling fish, to which the latter replied: 'there was no making fortunes now by fish'. Bristol was in the grip of a serious cholera epidemic,[4] exacerbated by the appalling state of the rivers and water supply, and this, combined with the effects of the rioting, had affected the economy.

In October, Rolinda numbered and arranged her sketches while Ellen and James Jnr were reading 'Mrs Trollop's Domestic Manners of America [Mrs Trollope's *Domestic Manners of the Americans*] with which Mr Ralston was so indignant' – referring back to their American visitor's stated disapproval of the book. Rolinda remarked on *Domestic Manners*:

> *It is very entertaining and well written but occasionally Mrs T. appears
> quite as vulgar as she represents some of the Americans. One of the plates
> is exceedingly vulgar ... Mrs T.'s description of a Senator's lady, and the
> Dorcas Society, is very entertaining.*

The intrepid Mrs Fanny Trollope, mother of the more famous Anthony, had been forced by financial hardship to write for a living. In 1832 she published *Domestic Manners*, one of the first travel books, relating her unfavourable impressions over several years in the fledgling Republic.[5] Always loyal to her former home, Ellen writes: 'Mrs T. offended every American reader'; the book was, however, a sensation in England.

By the end of 1832 Rolinda had 'introduced more than fifty persons into the Court Martial who have either sat to me at once in the picture or previously for sketches, they are not all finished'. As 1833 dawned, the year of her fortieth birthday, she ground her colours and sang glees at a small party, staying home later in the month to nurse a cold. Work on *The Trial* picture went on throughout the year,

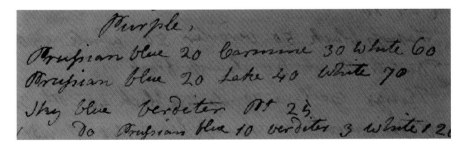

EXCERPT FROM ELLEN SHARPLES'S NOTEBOOK

with many of her sitters wanting copies of their portraits to keep. Some evenings were spent at musical parties and the occasional ball, and Rolinda's drive to educate herself continued unabated. She attended Mr Adam's paper on 'Optical Illusions' at the Institution as well as lectures in anatomy and zoology, studied Euclid with Miss Octavia Lemon and 'occasionally amused myself learning a little concology [conchology], Mr Stuchbury having been so obliging as to write most of the scientific names of my shells'.

A diagram identifying 46 of the (over 100) people portrayed in *The Trial* is displayed with the painting at M Shed (Bristol Museums), a record of many of the notable people of the time. Significantly, Rolinda had the self-assurance to include herself in the painting as a witness to the event. This was one of the first times a female artist had put her own self-portrait in the scene that she was recording; another rare, earlier, example being Clara Peeters, who in the seventeenth century had made herself visible in the shiny surfaces of the still-life objects she was painting.[6] Rolinda portrays herself working at her open sketchbook, while her mother is seated with her back to the viewer – although in fact Ellen had avoided going to the trial, disliking the crowds.

In January 1834 Rolinda 'began a new picture of the Rajah Ram Roy, from the picture for which [he] sat in the court martial'. Rajah Ram Mohan Roy had died in Bristol the previous September; he was an Indian social and religious reformer, known for his efforts to abolish the practices of sati (widow sacrifice) and child marriage. After a final series of sittings for *The Trial* and 'much company every day at 3 o'clock' she declared the painting finished on 24 February. The next day 'Miss Walton walked with us on the downs, quite fatigued talking to so much company … unable to speak except in a whisper … so hoarse as to be almost unable to speak.' Her friend Mr Corbin persuaded her to take some remedies, only to die himself a week later – much to Rolinda's shock. Despite Rolinda's cough, streams of visitors called to see the picture until, on 6 March, it was packed up and sent to London, to be exhibited at the Society of British Artists.

In May, after more portrait commissions, she resumed painting the *Clifton Racecourse* picture, working on it for the rest of the year. Many of her friends sat for the picture, and she also worked on several portraits in miniature, including, in January 1835: 'began another small picture for a brooch, the young Rajah [R.M. Roy] surrounded by young ladies'. She attended lectures on geology and fossil bones, despite wintry weather where the rain froze as it fell, with 'people slipping and falling much to the amusement of those safe at home'. Rolinda's interest in all forms of science was a constant throughout her life, and in fact the palaeontologist Mary Anning (1799–1847) had donated many of her important discoveries at Lyme Regis to the Bristol Institution.[7]

Election fever was again abroad, and Sir Richard Vyvyan, a Tory politician opposing Reform, and Philip Miles, a merchant banker and slave-owner from Leigh Court, were elected to Parliament. On 9 January Rolinda and Ellen went to see the procession of the 'blues' (perhaps the Royal Horse Guards, a cavalry regiment known as the Blues) in Bristol's Berkeley Square: 'very rainy and windy, the men had great difficulty in managing the flags, especially the large ones'.

## FINAL DAYS

One of Rolinda's last portraits was 'a kit kat portrait of my mother', which she started in January 1836 and worked on throughout the spring. This could well be the picture shown in Plate 5.1. Here, Ellen's expression is gentle but purposeful, and the light and shade of her elaborate gown and cloak is skilfully handled. The starched lace of her cap resembles a tiara, appropriate for the family matriarch, while the curled locks of the hair framing her face are still a rich brown, although Ellen is in her sixties. This may be daughterly flattery or perhaps artistic licence, as her portrayal of Colonel Brereton in *The Trial* is also as a young man, although he was aged fifty.

On 27 August Rolinda's final diary entry reads: 'stone laid for the new bridge, went to see the procession, crowds of people. Evening fireworks opposite St Vincent's Parade.' Rolinda and James, like their parents, were devotees of science and new inventions, and owned shares in the Clifton Suspension Bridge and the Great Western Railway. Just as work began on Brunel's bridge, which crossed their beloved Avon Gorge outside their window, Rolinda began to suffer from the illness which was to end her life. Ellen related these events in a letter to her friend Harriet Pigott:

> *My dear Rolinda, just as she was attaining perfection in her favourite art, a dark blighting cloud suddenly threw its shadow over all. A considerable induration in the right breast was perceived, the first manifestation of that most dreadful of all diseases, a cancer ... in a few months commenced a long and most painful illness, borne with a heroism beyond human nature.*

In the same letter, Ellen refers to Rolinda's portrait of Miss Pigott in the costume of Mary Queen of Scots, which she is about to send to her.

Rolinda was showered with gifts by her friends – 'whatever was likely to amuse was sent to her'. One friend with an especially comfortable carriage called every day to drive her slowly past the house, up and down beside the river until she tired.

Then, 'On the night of February 10th, 1838, to our inexpressible anguish she departed as if falling into a gentle and peaceful sleep.' In their grief James and Ellen took solace in each other's company, Ellen finding comfort in her son's unfailing attention. He made some beautiful drawings for Ellen to give to Rolinda's friends as a token of thanks for their great kindness during her illness. James's health was also delicate, and while at Lower Harley Place he suffered with an alarming cough. Although this had improved with the move to St Vincent's Parade, in the autumn of 1838 the cough returned, he became weaker and more emaciated, and, as Ellen wrote, 'on the 10th August 1839 he too departed, a year and a half after his sister, the dreadful blow was almost too great for me to sustain'.

Now aged seventy, Ellen continued to live beside the Avon at St Vincent's Parade, and became reconciled to her solitary life: 'One night in my waking hours I was endeavouring to enumerate the comforts that we daily experience. I had got to near 200 when I fell asleep.' Ellen spent time with her books, 'as much interested in some study as any schoolgirl', and found a kindred spirit at the other end of the Parade: a Mrs Lee who had fine paintings by Sir Thomas Lawrence. She corresponded with her friends and copied the letters and journals of different members of the family: 'three large scrapbooks are nearly filled with sketches and drawings, despite stooping position very unfavourable to my health'. Feeling adventurous, at the urging of Mrs Maze – who was 'partial to railroad conveyance' – she embarked on her first railway trip to Bath to visit a Miss S. After a journey of 21 minutes she took a fly to Bath's Prior Park in the rain, then back on the 7 o'clock in 28 minutes. In December 1844 Brunel's great iron ship the S.S. *Great Britain* passed her window en route to its first sea trials.

In 1844, an educator to the last and perhaps inspired by her visit of thirty years before to New York's first Academy of the Arts, Ellen donated the sum of £2,000 to a group of Trustees wishing to establish a Bristol Academy for the Promotion of the Fine Arts, to include a School of Painting and Sculpture. In January 1845 John Scandrett Harford, the venture's President, appealed for subscribers (Fig. 7). Harford, F.R.S., was a Quaker banker, abolitionist and friend of William Wilberforce, and his father had supported Hannah More's schools in Somerset. He announced that

> the munificence of a Bristol lady has prepared the way for the formation of
> an Academy of Painting ... Liverpool, Manchester and Birmingham have
> already founded similar institutions ... we must not be left behind in the career
> of intellectual improvement.

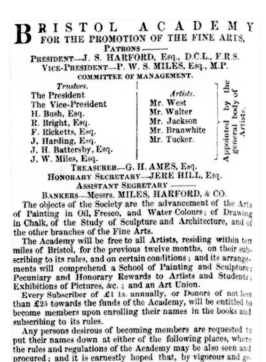

Fig. 7

An appeal for subscribers for Bristol's new arts academy, the *Bristol Mercury*, 18 January 1845.

Harford sought the advice of the President of London's Royal Academy at Burlington House, who advocated the establishment of life classes 'with strict rules on the observation of strict decorum'. Ironically, given the source of much of Ellen's wealth, he recommended the abolition of the practice of copying paintings on the grounds that such works were too abundant and tended to fill London's pawnbrokers' shops![8]

Artist members of the Bristol academy were to reside and practise within 10 miles of the city. The Duke of Beaufort, Earl Fitzharding and the Bishop of Bristol and Gloucester became patrons, as did Prince Albert, who sent a cheque for £25. Isambard Kingdom Brunel became an associate. The Bristol Institution for the Advancement of Science, Literature and the Arts agreed to lend its large room on Park Street for the Academy's exhibitions, and it was insisted that there should be equality of treatment between men and women painters.[9]

Art education was deemed to have foremost importance, and one of the earliest resolutions was to accept the offer of a room in Bristol's central Victoria Rooms (an assembly rooms and the most important concert venue in the West of England at the time) as the first drawing studio. Undoubtedly influenced by the gender of their benefactor, in 1845 separate life classes specially for women students were held there, arranged by a Mr M. Holmes at a shilling a time.[10]

It is quite possible that this was the first time that women had ever had access to life drawing as part of their formal training.

In Paris, the Ecole des Beaux-Arts enrolled female students in 1893, and in Germany women were not admitted to the academies in Berlin, Munich and Düsseldorf until after the 1910s and 20s. At America's first Academy of Art in Philadelphia, when mixed classes in drawing from plaster casts were introduced in 1856, tight-fitting fig leaves were attached to the statues to preserve the women's modesty. In 1860 an enthusiastic group of women students at the Philadelphia Academy, including Mary Cassatt, began to pose for each other until life classes for women were instituted in 1868.[11] Women students were excluded from the Royal Academy Schools in London until they were forced to open their doors in 1860, when the enterprising Laura Herford submitted a drawing signed only with her initials. Other female students followed but women were still barred from life classes until 1890.[12] Manchester's Academy did not admit women as members until the 1870s.

In her last years Ellen grew frail, but 'have just sufficient strength when the weather is favourable to walk up to the Crescent, Mall, Caledonia and Harley Place [in Clifton], where I have friends who receive me as cordially as ever'. She was cared for by her faithful servant Maria Johnson, who had replaced her sister on her marriage 18 years before. Ellen's relationship with Maria was reflected in a legacy of £500 in her will, enough to keep her in comfort for the rest of her life. An attack of St Anthony's Fire – erysipelas – caused pain in her right arm but after a month she was conveyed to Clifton in a wheelchair, an experience the independent Ellen disliked:

> *I shall probably in time be reconciled to the cushioned sofa … regaining a little strength, the wheelchair not to my taste, was soon dismissed, and I have since every fine day regularly walked out, and two or three times, with my walking parasol, mounted the hill as far as the Crescent and Caledonia Place.*

Anyone who knows the steepness of the hill from the riverside up to Clifton cannot but admire her spirit.

On 14 March 1849, at the age of eighty, Ellen's exceptional life came to an end. She was buried with some ceremony beside her beloved son and daughter at Clifton Parish Church: the graveyard remains there at Birdcage Walk, at the time of writing an overgrown tangle of brambles. In her will she added to her previous gift by bequeathing over £4,000, together with her family's art collection of 97 pictures, to the Bristol Academy, now the Royal West of England Academy (RWA), ensuring the future of that institution in the beautiful building which opened in Clifton in 1858 and still flourishes there today.

Ellen and her daughter Rolinda, two strong, spirited and independent women, carved out a position in the history of art which deserves recognition. For Ellen, coming from a working-class family, to achieve international success as an artist before there was any public conception that women had a serious contribution to make in the fine arts, makes her one of the pioneers of the women's art movement. Previously regarded solely as a copyist of her husband's portraits, it is now apparent that she forged her own career, producing many fine works with an original style of her own. Her writings as an educated and cultured woman reflect her unusual and impressive life, as she combined the roles of artist, wife and mother, in an environment that was deeply hostile to the progression of women, while never losing her love of learning.

Ellen's patronage of the Bristol Academy was vital to the national development of art education and in creating a space for future artists. She was a mentor for her daughter Rolinda, who produced a significant body of work despite a lack of formal training or any acknowledgement by the art establishment until late in life: 'Although strictly speaking a Georgian artist … she seems now in retrospect a prototype of the female artists who arose from the generations succeeding her.'[13] In having the ambition to make pictures reflecting the social and political events of her time, Rolinda increased the range of possibilities open to female artists in the future.

On 24 March 1849 the *Bristol Mercury* published Ellen's obituary: 'Her memory deserves to be cherished by every lover of the fine arts in this city as long as Bristol endures.' In August of that year the Sharples Gallery opened, admission sixpence, at the Academy's first premises at 18 St Augustine's Parade, alongside the annual exhibition of works by living artists.[14] The legacy of these inspiring women lives on.

For
The Bristol Academy.
Ellen Sharples.

# Notes

General note: Quotations and other material from the Sharples journal and other Sharples papers are not cited here. See the Bibliography for sources.

## INTRODUCTION

1. Fine Arts Gallery, Independence National Historical Park, Philadelphia, online portrait collection, https://museum.nps.gov
2. See http://museums.bristol.gov.uk

## CHAPTER 1: BEGINNINGS, MARRIAGE AND ARTISTIC ADVENTURES IN AMERICA, 1780s–1801

1. *Cumberland Pacquet, and Ware's Whitehaven Advertiser*, 21 June 1786
2. Knox, K. McC, *The Sharples: Their Portraits of George Washington and His Contemporaries* (Yale University Press, 1930), p.5, and correspondence with Marian Clarke at Frick Art Reference Library, May 2019
3. Knox, *The Sharples*, p.5
4. Brown, David Blayney, *Ashmolean Museum Oxford: Catalogue of the Collection of Drawings*, IV: *The Earlier British Drawings: British Artists and Foreigners Working in Britain Born before c.1775* (Clarendon Press, 1982)
5. Knox, *The Sharples*, p.3
6. Jeffares. N., *Dictionary of Pastellists before 1800*, online at www.pastellists.com/Articles/Sharples.pdf
7. Nicholson, W., *Journal of Natural Philosophy*, vol. VII, 1804, 'Description of an Apparatus for Raising Water by the Fall of Waste Water', by Mr Sharples, Portrait Painter, Bath; Pamphlet of Specification, of James Sharples, 'Reducing Friction in Machinery' (1791), reprinted 1856; Pamphlet of Specification, of James Sharples, 'Steam Engines, Etc' (1802), reprinted 1855 (the above pamphlets printed by Eyre and Spottiswoode, published at the Great Seal Patent Office, 15 Southampton Building, Holborn, London); Specification of James Sharples (A.D. 1804), 'Apparatus for Surveying etc', Patent No. 2794 (Science Museum, London, Records). Of a mathematical table used in one of his inventions Sharples states: 'this rule is so easy in its application that my daughter, Rolinda, a child of eleven years old, can answer any question relative to this combination, extending to a cycle of 999,900, almost as soon as she can write down the figures'; Hosack, D., and Francis, J.W., *The American Medical and Philosophical Register*, April 1811, 'An Investigation of the Principles of Steam Carriage, Communicated to the Editors by the Late James Sharples Esq. Full page drawing facing p.421 by J.S. of Mr Trevithick's carriage and engine'; *London Courier and Evening Gazetteer*, 14 November 1805, published in a list of patents for inventions: 'Mr Sharples for Implements for Measuring Distances'

8. *Collected Letters of Robert Southey, Part 2*, 12 July 1799, online at romantic-circles.org, section number 421

9. *Bath Chronicle*, 11 August 1791

10. *Bath Chronicle*, 7 November 1793

11. *Bath Chronicle*, 3 October 1793

12. Dunlap, W., *The History of the Rise and Progress of the Arts of Design in the United States*, vol. 2, 1834 (Dover Publications, 1969), pp.70–71

13. Uglow, J., *Elizabeth Gaskell* (Faber and Faber, 1999), p.29

14. Letter to R.B. Ward from Philip Miles, 25 September 1845, Bristol Archives

15. *Bath Chronicle*, 10 April 1794

16. *Bath Chronicle*, 4 September 1794

17. Diary of William Dunlap, 1766–1839, online at archive.org; entries in diary for 1797–8 refer to Sharples

18. Fanelli, D., and Diethorn, K., *History and Catalog of the Portrait Collection, Independence National Historical Park* (American Philosophical Society, Independence Square, Philadelphia, 2001)

19. Baetjer, K., and Shelley, M., *Pastel Portraits: Images of 18th-century Europe*, adapted from *The Metropolitan Museum of Art Bulletin*, vol. 68 no. 4, Spring 2011, p.42

20. Baetjer and Shelley, *Pastel Portraits*

21. Palmer, J.W., *Lippincott's Magazine*, December 1871

22. Stoddard, S., 'The Sharples Family', in Sansom, J., ed., *Public View: A Profile of the Royal West of England Academy* (Redcliffe Press, 2002), p.25

23. Liancourt (1747–1827) was a social reformer who fled to the US during the French Revolution, a few days before his cousin was stoned to death. He wrote about his extensive travels, including in the country of the Iroquois, and we might speculate that he may have brought back the image Ellen used as the source for her watercolour-on-ivory of a Native American chief (Plate 2.1). He saw Washington being built in 1797, making a small town of 5,000 into the capital city. See La Rochefoucauld-Liancourt, François-Alexandre-Frédéric, Duc de, trans. Henry Neuman, *Travels through the United States of North America, the Country of the Iroquois, and Upper Canada in the Years 1795, 1796, and 1797; with an Authentic Account of Lower Canada* (R. Phillips, 1799), online at https://lccn.loc.gov/01024772. Also Brandenburg, D.J., and Brandenberg, M.H., 'The Duc de la Rochefoucauld-Liancourt's Visit to the Federal City in 1797: A New Translation', *Records of the Columbia Historical Society*, 49, 1973–4, pp.35–60.

24. Palmer, *Lippincott's Magazine*, December 1871

25. Knox, *The Sharples*, p.15

26. Miles, E.G., *Saint-Mémin and the Neoclassical Profile Portrait in America* (National Portrait Gallery/Smithsonian, 1994)

27. Chernow, R., *Alexander Hamilton* (Head of Zeus Ltd, 2016), p.181

28. Knox, *The Sharples*, p.15

29. *New York City Directory*, 1798, online at https://digitalcollections.nypl.org

## CHAPTER 2: BATH, BRISTOL AND BACK TO AMERICA, 1801–9

1. Pointon, M., '"Surrounded with Brilliants": Miniature Portraits in Eighteenth-century England', *The Art Bulletin*, vol. 83 no. 1, March 2001, pp.48–71

2. See emuseum.mountvernon.org

3. Borzello, F., *Seeing Ourselves: Women's Self-portraits* (Thames and Hudson, 2018), p.105

4. Waller, S., *Women Artists in the Modern Era: A Documentary History* (The Scarecrow Press Inc., 1991), p.42

5. Hamilton, A. McL., *The Intimate Life of Alexander Hamilton* (Duckworth, 1911), pp.32–3

6. Graves, A., *The Royal Academy of Arts: A Complete Dictionary of Contributors and Their Work from Its Foundation in 1769 to 1904* (H. Graves and Co., 1905), p.93

7. See, for example, Saint-Mémin's *Osage Warrier*, at www.metmuseum.org

8. Stoddard, S., 'The Sharples Family', in Sansom, J., ed., in *Public View: A Profile of the Royal West of England Academy* (Redcliffe Press, 2002), p.28

9. Correspondence with Jonathan Lainey, Curator, Indigenous Cultures, McCord Museum, Montreal. He compares these with similar crosses in their collection made as trade goods by silversmith Charles Arnoldi, active in Montreal 1779–1817

## CHAPTER 3: SECOND AMERICAN VISIT AND JAMES'S DEATH, 1809–11

1. Fanelli, D., and Diethorn, K., *History and Catalog of the Portrait Collection, Independence National Historical Park* (American Philosophical Society, Philadelphia, 2001), p.237

2. Knox, K. McC, *The Sharples: Their Portraits of George Washington and His Contemporaries* (Yale University Press, 1930), p.40

3. Fanelli and Diethorn, *History and Catalog of the Portrait Collection*, p.67

4. Diethorn, K., 'Peale's Philadelphia Museum', in *The Encyclopedia of Greater Philadelphia*, online at philadelphiaencyclopedia.org

5. Museum of Early Southern Decorative Arts, Winston-Salem, North Carolina, has works by Felix Sharples that can be seen online at www.mesda.org/lp/collection/paintings; his work is also at the Chrysler Museum of Art, Norfolk, Virginia, online at www.chrysler.org/art/collection

6. Fanelli and Diethorn, *History and Catalog of the Portrait Collection*, p.43

7. Knox, *The Sharples*, p.49, and Hunt, A., 'Notes on Felix Thomas Sharples', *The Virginia Magazine of History and Biography*, vol. 59 no. 2, April 1951, pp.216–24

8. The Bank of England issued these share certificates to pay off debts incurred by the British Navy, in return for an annuity at the relatively high rate of 5 per cent. The rate was considerably reduced during the 1820s – one of the reasons why Ellen rented on St Vincent's Parade rather than buying in Clifton in 1831 (see Chapter 5)

## CHAPTER 4: BRISTOL, LONDON AND RECOGNITION FOR ROLINDA, 1811–20s

1. Borzello, F., *Seeing Ourselves: Women's Self-portraits* (Thames and Hudson, 2018), p.116

2. Gerrish Nunn, P., *Victorian Women Artists* (Women's Press, 1987), p.69

3. Letter to Mrs Grace Davy, 11 October 1798, online at www.davy-letters.org.uk

4. John Draper, *Somerset, with the Severn Sea: A Poem, with Historical and Miscellaneous Notes* (1867), quoted in Greenacre, F., *The Bristol School of Artists: Francis Danby and Painting in Bristol 1810–1840* (City Art Gallery, Bristol, 1973), p.18

5. B.M. [British Museum] MS 36512, vol. XXII, f.156, 3 December 1827, quoted in Greenacre, F., *The Bristol School of Artists*, p.211

6. For Ellen's recipe for plumb cake and advice on dressing a turtle, see Appendix

7. Borzello, F., *Seeing Ourselves*, p.99, and Farington, J., *Diary 1793–1821*, 8 vols, ed. J. Greig (Hutchinson & Co., 1922). *The Farington Diary* is also available online at archive.org

8. Greenacre, F., *The Bristol School of Artists*, p.108

9. Yeldham, C., *Maria Spilsbury (1776–1820): Artist and Evangelical* (Routledge, 2010)

10. Wray, N., Curator, University of Bristol Botanic Garden, see 'A Portrait of a Boy and a Plant', botanic-garden.bristol.ac.uk, posted 14 February 2017

11. See bonhams.com, 23 November 2005, lot 121

12. See bonhams.com, 23 November 2005, lot 120

13. See bonhams.com, 9 March 2004, lot 31

14. See bonhams.com, 8 March 2005, lot 40

15. See bonhams.com, 8 March 2005, lot 41

16. See bonhams.com, 8 November 2005, lot 112

17. See www.milesbarton.com, Sold Archive

18. See bonhams.com, 23 November 2011, lot 161

19. Sotheby's, 14 October 2003

20. Christie's, 2 September 2008, lot 163

21. See www.thecanterburyauctiongalleries.com, 14 April 2015, lot 381

22. See bonhams.com, 9 March 2004

23. *Bristol Mercury*, 23 January 1836

24. Royal Academy listing of exhibitors, in Graves, A., *The Royal Academy of Arts: A Complete Dictionary of Contributors and Their Work from Its Foundation in 1769 to 1904* (Henry Graves & Co. Ltd and George Bell & Sons, 1905–6), p.93

25. Sotheby's, 15 July 1992, lot 85

26. *John Bull*, 12 May 1822

27. See www.artwarefineart.com, oil on canvas, £2,000 (accessed 21 June 2021)

28. Christie's, 4 July 2012, lot 149

29. Greenacre, F., *The Bristol School of Artists*, p.213

## CHAPTER 5: ROLINDA AND ELLEN'S LATER YEARS, LATE 1820s–49

1. Havemann, A., 'Expanded Horizon: Female Artists at the Pennsylvania Academy of the Fine Arts during the Course of the Nineteenth Century', in *The Female Gaze: Women Artists Making Their World*, ed. Robert Cozzolino (Pennsylvania Academy of the Fine Arts, 2012)

2. Barry, F.V., ed., *Maria Edgeworth: Chosen Letters* (Jonathan Cape, 1931), p.47

3. Metz, K., 'Ellen and Rolinda Sharples: Mother and Daughter Painters', *Woman's Art Journal*, vol. 16 no. 1, Spring/Summer 1995, footnote 38.

4. Hardiman, S., 'The 1832 Cholera Epidemic and Its impact on the City of Bristol', pamphlet from the Bristol branch of the Historical Association, online at www.bris.ac.uk

5. Trollope, F.M., *Domestic Manners of the Americans* ([1832], Oxford University Press, 2014)

6. Rideal, L., and Soriano, K., *Madam and Eve: Women Portraying Women* (Laurence King, 2018), p.10

7. Hutchinson, D., Curator, Geology, Bristol Museum and Art Gallery, 'The Bristol Institution and Mary Anning, a Pioneering Palaeontologist', www.bristolmuseums.org.uk, posted 16 April 2021

8. Milner D., *The Royal West of England Academy Bristol: An Essay in Patronage* (The Council of the RWA, c.1985), p.5

9. Milner, *The Royal West of England Academy*, p.5

10. Milner, *The Royal West of England Academy*, p.9

11. Havemann, 'Expanded Horizon'

12. Wickham A., Curator, Works on Paper, Royal Academy, 'A "Female Invasion" 250 Years in the Making', www.royalacademy.org.uk, posted 13 May 2018

13. Gerrish Nunn, P., *Victorian Women Artists* (Women's Press, 1987), p. 71.

14. *Bristol Times and Mirror*, 11 August 1849

# Appendix

These are taken from Ellen Sharples's book of notes and recipes. It is not always clear what she means by some terms; she was probably using them in her own, or a then-popular, way and also her spelling of them varies.

## TO MAKE A GOOD PLUMB CAKE

Take a pound and a half of fine flour well dried, a pound and a half of butter, 3 quarters of a pound of currants washed and well picked, stone half a pound of raisins and slice them, 18 ounces of sugar beat and sifted, 14 eggs, leave out half the whites, shred the peel of a large lemon exceeding fine, 3 ounces of candied orange, the same of lemon, a teaspoonful of beaten mace, half a nutmeg grated, a teacupful of brandy or white wine, 4 spoonsful of orange flower water; first work the butter with your hand to cream, then beat your sugar well in, whisk your eggs for half an hour, then mix them with your sugar and butter and put in your flour and spices, when your oven is ready, mix your brandy, fruit and sweetmeats lightly in, then put it in your hoop, and send it to the oven, it will require 2 hours and a half baking, it will take an hour and a half beating.

## TO DRESS A TURTLE ABOUT THIRTY POUNDS WEIGHT

When you kill the turtle, which must be done the night before, cut off the head and let it bleed two or three hours. Then cut off the fins and the calliper from the calabash, take care you do not burst the gall, throw all the inwards [innards] into cold water, the guts and tripe keep by themselves and slit them open with a penknife and wash them very clean in scalding water.

Scrape off the inwards skin, as you do them throw them into cold water, wash them out of that and put them into fresh water and let them lie all night, scalding the fins and edges of the callipash and calliper; cut the meat off the shoulders and hack the bones, and set them over the fire with the fins in about a quart of water.

Put in a little mace, nutmeg, chian and salt, let it stew about three hours, then strain it and put the fins by for use, the next morning take some of the meat you cut off the shoulders and chop it as small as for sausages, with a pound of beef or veal suet, seasoned with mace, nutmeg, sweet marjoram, parsley, chyan and salt to your taste, and three or four glasses of madeira wine, so stuff it under the two fleshy parts of the meat and if you have any left, lay it over to prevent the meat from burning, then cut the remainder of the meat and the fins in pieces the size of an egg, season it pretty high with chyan, salt and a little nutmeg and put it into the cali-pash, take care it be sewed or secured up at the ends to keep in the gravy, then boil up the gravy and add more wine if required, and thicken it with butter and flour, put some of it to the turtle, and set it in the oven with a well buttered paper over it to keep it from burning, and when it is about half baked squeeze in the juice of one or two lemons and stir it up.

Callipash or back will take half an hour more baking than the callipee, which two hours will do; the guts may be cut in pieces two or three inches long, the tripe in less and put into a mug of clear water and set it in the oven with the calipash, and when it is enough and drained from the water, it is to be mixed with the other parts and put up very hot.

ELLEN SHARPLES'S PLUMB CAKE

# Bibliography

All quotations throughout the book have been taken from Ellen Sharples's journal, which includes Rolinda's diary entries, or from Sharples family correspondence/papers, unless otherwise stated; sources: Ellen Sharples's journal/diary, 1803–36, and Ellen Sharples's letter book, 1836–49, and related papers: Bristol Archives, B Bond Warehouse, Smeaton Road, Bristol BS1 6XN.

Some other quotes and material not cited in the book's Notes section, including photographs of Ellen's handwritten notes on paint preparation and colour-mixing, and the items in the Appendix, are sourced from Ellen Sharples's book of notes and recipes: RWA (Royal West of England Academy, Bristol), Library item no. 37.

Baetjer, K., and Shelley, M., *Pastel Portraits: Images of 18th-century Europe*, adapted from *The Metropolitan Museum of Art Bulletin*, vol. 68 no. 4, Spring 2011, pp.4–56

Barry, F.V., ed., *Maria Edgeworth: Chosen Letters* (Jonathan Cape, 1931)

Bolton, T., *Early American Portrait Draughtsmen in Crayons* (F.F. Sherman, 1923)

Borzello, F., *Seeing Ourselves: Women's Self-portraits* (Thames and Hudson, 2018)

Brandenburg, D. and M., 'The Duc de la Rochefoucauld-Liancourt's Visit to the Federal City in 1797: A New Translation', *Records of the Columbia Historical Society, Washington, D.C.*, vol. 49 (1973), pp.35–60; available online at www.jstor.org/stable/40067734

Chernow, R., *Alexander Hamilton* (Head of Zeus Ltd, 2016)

Dunlap, W., *The History of the Rise and Progress of the Arts of Design in the United States* ([1834] Dover Publications, 1969)

Dunlap, W., and Barck, D., ed. and transcriber, *Diary of William Dunlap (1766–1839): The Memoirs of a Dramatist, Theatrical Manager, Painter, Critic, Novelist and Historian* (printed for New York Historical Society, 1930). Entries in diary for 1797–8 refer to Sharples; available online at archive.org

Fanelli, D., and Diethorn, K., *History and Catalog of the Portrait Collection, Independence National Historical Park* (American Philosophical Society, Philadelphia, 2001)

Farington, J., *Diary 1793–1821*, 8 vols, ed. J. Greig (Hutchinson & Co., 1922). *The Farington Diary* is also available online at archive.org

Gerrish Nunn, P., *Victorian Women Artists* (Women's Press, 1987)

Graves, A., *The Royal Academy of Arts: A Complete Dictionary of Contributors and Their Work from Its Foundation in 1769 to 1904* (Henry Graves & Co. Ltd and George Bell & Sons, 1905–6)

Greenacre, F., *The Bristol School of Artists: Francis Danby and Painting in Bristol 1810–1840* (City Art Gallery Bristol, 1973)

Hamilton, A. McL., *The Intimate Life of Alexander Hamilton* (Duckworth, 1911), pp.32–3

Havemann, A., 'Expanded Horizon: Female Artists at the Pennsylvania Academy of the Fine Arts during the Course of the Nineteenth Century', in *The Female Gaze: Women Artists Making Their World*, ed. Robert Cozzolino (Pennsylvania Academy of the Fine Arts, 2012)

Jeffares, N., *Dictionary of Pastellists before 1800* (Unicorn Press, 2006); available online at www.pastellists.com

Knox, K. McC., *The Sharples: Their Portraits of George Washington and His Contemporaries* (Yale University Press, 1930)

Metz, K., 'Ellen and Rolinda Sharples: Mother and Daughter Painters', *Woman's Art Journal*, vol. 16 no. 1, Spring/Summer 1995, pp.3–11

Miles, E.G., *Saint-Mémin and the Neoclassical Profile Portrait in America* (National Portrait Gallery/Smithsonian, 1994)

Milner D., *The Royal West of England Academy Bristol: An Essay in Patronage* (The Council of the RWA, *c.*1985)

Pevsner. N., *Academies of Art Past and Present* (Da Capo Press, 1973)

Quick, R., *Catalogue (with Biographical Notes and Illustrations) of the Sharples Collection of Pastel Portraits and Oil Paintings, etc.* (Bristol Art Gallery, 1900); available online at https://library.si.edu

Rideal, L., and Soriano, K., *Madam and Eve: Women Portraying Women* (Laurence King, 2018)

Sansom, J., ed., *Public View: A Profile of the Royal West of England Academy* (Redcliffe Press, 2002)

Steeds, M., and Ball, R., *From Wulfstan to Colston: Severing the Sinews of Slavery in Bristol* (Bristol Radical History Group, 2020)

Trollope, F.M., *Domestic Manners of the Americans* ([1832], Oxford University Press, 2014)

Waggoner, D., *The Sharples Collection: Family and Legal Papers 1794–1854* (Microform Academic Publishers, 2001)

Waller, S., *Women Artists in the Modern Era: A Documentary History* (The Scarecrow Press Inc., 1991)

Wickham, A., Curator, Works on Paper, Royal Academy, 'A "Female Invasion" 250 Years in the Making', www.royalacademy.org.uk, posted 13 May 2018

Wray, N., Curator, University of Bristol Botanic Garden, see 'A Portrait of a Boy and a Plant', botanic-garden.bristol.ac.uk, posted 14 February 2017

Yeldham, C., *Maria Spilsbury (1776–1820): Artist and Evangelical* (Routledge, 2010)

# Author's Acknowledgements

The book was originally inspired by a script for a film about Rolinda Sharples for HTV West in 1996. I'd like to thank the cast and crew: Toyah Willcox, P.J. Crook, Jenny Falconer, Jill Ranford, Nick Turner, Jayne Chard, and especially Lee Cox, without whose encouragement the book would not have happened.

Thanks to Abigail Davies for all her support for previous independent films about women artists whose work remains hidden, and to Sue Giles for her wise advice.

At the RWA, Alison Bevan's interest and enthusiasm carried the idea forward, and Tristan Pollard is always a tower of strength.

The help and advice of the staff at Bristol Museum and Art Gallery, especially Jenny Gaschke, Kate Newnham and Trevor Coombs, and the staff at Bristol and Bath Archives, has been invaluable and greatly appreciated. Also Marian Clarke at the Frick Art Reference Library in New York and, in Philadelphia, PA: Hoang Tran at Pennsylvania Academy of the Fine Arts and Karie Diethorn at Independence National Historical Park.

Many thanks to Clara Hudson at Redcliffe Press for believing in the book, and to Ann Kay and Melinda Welch for contributing such knowledge and expertise; thanks also for Jon Rowley's brilliant photography.

I thank my wonderful family for all their love and support and putting up with me boring them senseless with tales of the Sharples family. Special thanks to Colin, whose interest and encouragement were unwavering and made everything possible.

# Select Index